FIRST
IN THIS LAND

VOICES AND VERSE FROM NAXIYAMTÁMA (SNAKE RIVER-PALOUSE) AND OTHER COLUMBIA PLATEAU TRIBAL ELDERS

FIRST
IN THIS LAND

VOICES AND VERSE FROM
NAXIYAMTÁMA (SNAKE RIVER-PALOUSE)
AND OTHER COLUMBIA PLATEAU
TRIBAL ELDERS

EDITED BY
CLIFFORD E. TRAFZER / TSEMINIKUM
AND
RICHARD D. SCHEUERMAN / WOWEEIK

FOREWORD BY
MALISSA MINTHORN / WIYÁAPALASONMI
ILLUSTRATIONS BY
JEREMY WOLF / XALISH WASHUMKI

Triticum Press
Pasco, Washington

FIRST IN THIS LAND:
Voices and Verse from *Naxiyamtáma* (Snake River-Palouse) and
Other Columbia Plateau Tribal Elders

Copyright 2025, First Printing
Introduction and Part II © 2025 Clifford E. Trafzer and
    Richard D. Scheuerman
Part I selections reprinted with permission of the contributors
Pen and ink illustrations by Jeremy Wolf
Includes bibliographical references and index

This is a publication of Triticum Press
9903 Coronado Dr
Pasco, Washington 99301

Design: Carol O'Callaghan, Triticum Press
Cover Image Composite: Lee Moorhouse "Thorn Hollow Looking East"
    (c. 1910) Courtesy Tamastslikt Cultural Institute

PAPERBACK ISBN: 979-8-9928914-0-9
Library of Congress Control Number: 2025933954

This book is published with grant support from the
Rupert and Jeanette Costco Endowment for
American Indian Affairs
University of California-Riverside

Royalties from this publication support non-profit
educational programs of the Confederated Tribes of the
Umatilla Indian Reservation's Tamastsklikt Cultural Institute.

Chapter Epigraphs:
Natalie Pond, Palouse-Umatilla Beaded Medallion (2005)
Columbia Plateau Center for American Indian Studies
Washington State University, Pullman

We respectfully dedicate this work to
Malissa Minthorn / Wiyáapalasonmi
Roberta "Bobbie" Conner / Stsaawipam
and Marjorie Waheneka / Et-twaii-lish

He put our bodies here in this land,
  and everything across the west toward the
  sunset. . . .
We were first in this land
  and then the last ones on the left hand,
   on the sunset side.

       —Atilapum Minthorn,
    "How Coyote Made the River Flow"

CONTENTS

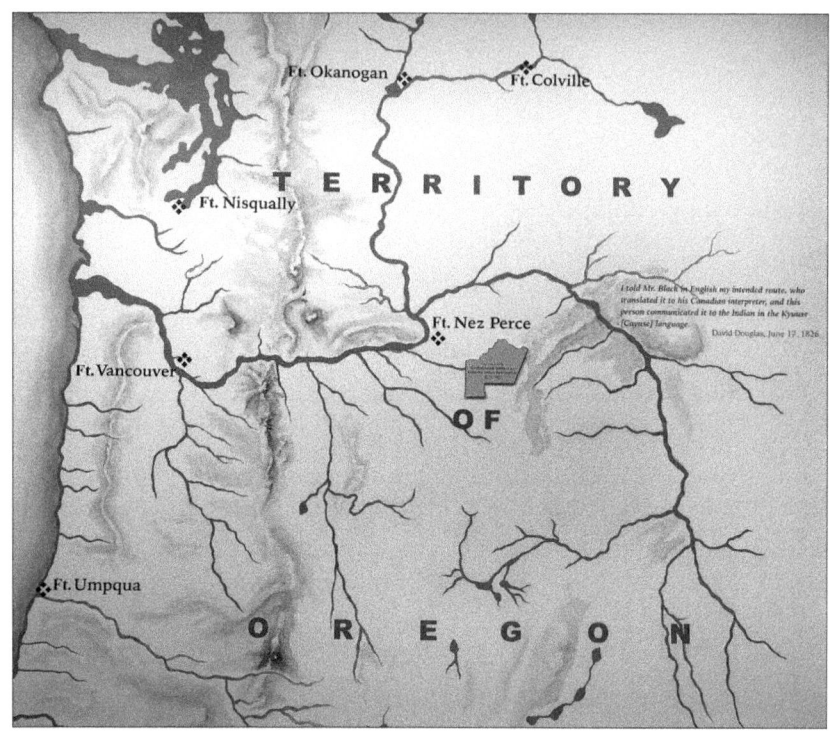

The Oregon Territory and Umatilla Indian Reservation Map
"Picturing Family: Métis Life in the Walla Walla Valley" Exhibit
Courtesy Historic Frenchtown Foundation

FOREWORD

If the general public is to better understand our worlds close at hand and beyond, it is necessary for historians to study, interpret, and advance informed understandings. The editors and contributors to this collection of oral histories and articles have been instrumental in accomplishing these important tasks. Among our Confederated Tribes of the Umatilla Indian Reservation are many families of Snake River-Palouse heritage who relocated here after the 1855 Walla Walla Council Treaties. Some of them remained well into the twentieth century in their ancestral homeland, which stretched from the confluence of the Snake and Yakima Rivers with the Columbia far to the east to Nez Perce country. Since time immemorial they followed the seasonal round across the Palouse Hills to gather traditional foods, to hunt there and in the surrounding mountains, and to fish in the clear waters of the Palouse, Tucannon, Snake, Columbia, and other rivers. The ancient teachings of these people and others with whom they joined here on the Umatilla Reservation are paramount to our wellbeing and to our lands and waters.

Clifford Trafzer and Richard Scheuerman have recorded many of these truths that our elders affirmed through oral histories since they began visiting among us four decades ago. They patiently and respectfully listened, learned, and shared with later generations the fruits of their labors, and their contributions have significantly added to our Tamástslikt Cultural Institute Library and Archives. Their work, in turn, built upon the dedicated efforts of historians Robert Ruby and John Brown that also enhanced our collections and exhibits. I came to this work in the 1990s after experiences both on and off the reservation. My father was among tribal members who were encouraged to take part in the 1950s Bureau of Indian Affairs relocation program when the federal government did not yet consider us full citizens. We were sent with others to California but soon discovered that the promised jobs, homes, and opportunities did not exist. Our families struggled and managed to make it back north only as far as Portland. Like many others of my generation, I came of age amidst news of Wounded Knee, the Alcatraz Occupation, and the Fish-In protests at Frank's Landing among the Nisqually.

While this period of Indigenous activism drew national attention to American Indian causes, I joined my family on regular trips "back home" to the Umatilla Reservation to take part in traditional feasts, memorials, the Pendleton Round-Up, and to hunt and fish. In these ways I came to first know the places that surround our reservation. From friends and family members, I came to understand the historic trauma experienced by Indian people. My father decided to return to the reservation in the 1970s where he became active in tribal politics and worked to preserve cultural knowledge through language and history projects. For some time I went back and forth, east and west, between the city and country life on the reservation. I came to appreciate more and more the land and people of my heritage. I soon realized that I could never go back to urban living.

Young women like me had limited opportunities even in the relatively modern times of the 1980s. I attended Blue Mountain Community College in Pendleton and began work for the tribe as a community health representative, which introduced me to a wider circle of elders beyond my family and friends. In this way I came to know many elders who lived in places like Thorn Hollow and Cayuse who are represented in this book and who maintained their ancestral ways amidst the pace of change in the world around them. Later in the decade I worked in tribal administration as federal property and supply program supervisor and for the Forest Service, which introduced me to cultural resource management. These were the years that Richard and Clifford were working on their book *Renegade Tribe* (1986) about the Snake

River-Palouse people that led to their first visits here with members of the Wolf, Patrick, Thompson, Johnley, and other families.

In 1992, I came on staff to what was called the Oregon Trail Interpretive Center of Umatilla Indian Reservation that was the forerunner of the Támastslikt Cultural Institute. At that time, a national effort was underway to commemorate the 150th anniversary of the Oregon Trail in 1993. I hoped that I had sufficient knowledge and experience to take on these important new responsibilities. I spoke with my grandmother about the challenges since so much of what was presented in area museums, on highway signage, and in books was told from the prevailing dominant perspective of the Westward Movement. We recognized the significance of the historic Oregon Trail route but were weary of others trying to tell our story. My grandmother said, "The Creator puts us where He wants us to be." I listened to what she said and have been here ever since in tribute to her. Under Bobbie Conner's leadership we have sought to go beyond preservation of objects and records to tell our story as the living experience that it is with vital lessons for personal wellbeing, tribal identity, and care for the land.

Our people have long expressed essential understandings about regard for each other and for the land through story, song, and art. A critical piece of this effort has been to keep our cultural knowledge pure and intact through the gathering and preservation of oral histories. We live in an age of substantial misinformation when false claims and opinion are presented as facts and knowledge. We appreciate the efforts of historians like Clifford and Richard to build trusting relationships over many years that document important aspects of our history and culture as related by our elders. They have also brought to our collections sources they have gleaned from their work on other reservations and from archives elsewhere in the nation.

Through oral histories such as those featured in this collection we have been able to reacquaint ourselves today with special knowledge that might have been lost. How remarkable Gilbert Minthorn's opening account is of sacred *Yamústas* and happenings that took place before the Missoula Floods many thousands of years ago. Nowhere on earth do written records exist from such ancient pasts, and yet here among our people these stories testify to our presence in the region down through the ages. Certainly there are lessons all can learn from such experience that could inform current public debate on issues ranging from salmon recovery to ethical leadership.

In these and other ways Clifford and Richard have worked with us to help tear down longstanding boundaries of inquiry and "old citation" misconceptions to present fuller understandings for all who might seek "the Indian side of the story." In 2001, I attended the Western Archives Institute's first Tribal Archives Conference at the University of Redlands in California where I met Clifford. I had known of his work with Richard on *Renegade Tribe* but he also shared with me their extensive *Yakama, Palouse, Cayuse, Umatilla, Walla Walla, and Wanapum Indians Bibliography*. That book opened the door to a number of original sources that informed work we were doing to build our library collection. It also led to further visits between them and Dr. Ruby with tribal elders and gatherings sponsored by Tamástslikt. In these ways, we continue to undertake projects like *First in This Land* as important steps in our unfolding mission to honor the elders by sharing their wisdom and experience to benefit the next generation. My grandmother also said, "The Creator has a plan." May we all strive to find our place within it.

Malissa Minthorn/Wiyáapalasonmi, Archivist and Librarian
Tamástslikt Cultural Institute
Pendleton, Oregon

PREFACE

The voices of *Naxiyamtáma* (Snake River-Palouse), Umatilla, Cayuse, and Walla Walla peoples are as old as time. For generations these peoples learned their history, religion, and culture through the oral tradition. The first literature of North, South, and Central America survived through the voices of Indigenous elders who passed along knowledge, insights, and experiences. The use of oral history to remember the past and prepare for the future required speaking, listening, and remembering. These were skills highly valued among Snake River-Palouse people. Learning through oral stories was once common among the first peoples of the Western Hemisphere—also known as the Native Universe. Native Americans have long used the oral tradition as a means of communicating knowledge, information intended to be shared with future generations.

The oral tradition offered a method of knowing and remembering, which has lived for many generations. Oral history remains alive among many Indigenous people, including the Snake River-Palouse. It is also one method we have used for nearly fifty years in their community-based academic work. Learning from elders and tribal scholars is the hallmark of the historical and cultural field of Palouse Studies. In addition to researching documents and information in libraries, archives, historical societies, and personal collections, we listened to and learned from Palouse elders and reservation scholars who gifted us with their knowledge and histories. We are forever indebted to them for sharing their knowledge.

We have learned that elders select their words carefully because words matter. As one tribal elder explained, "In life we have only so many breaths, and we must not waste them." Words inform and carry power. Scholars must take seriously the words of knowledgeable tribal

xvii

people. We considered their words carefully and use them as part of our analysis of the Palouse past. Spoken words have power and force, not to be taken lightly. The *Naxiyamtáma* of the lower Snake River know their history, culture, religion, and geography. They have contributed a great deal to our work and this present study, *First in This Land*.

Snake River-Palouse elders we have known understood the significance of the spoken word within their communities and other Indigenous communities. Since the time of creation, they had used oral traditions as their way of recording the past and teaching their young people. Palouse parents, grandparents, uncles, and aunts taught their children through the oral tradition, repeating the same stories again and again the same ways. Children heard the stories for years. Then one day, elders would ask a child to be the storyteller and share one of the accounts they had heard so often. Elders oversaw the education of young people in this way. They taught children to listen as they taught the history of their people. They spent a great deal of time explaining the importance of places, including places with positive and negative energy. They imparted wisdom, knowledge, and power in the spoken word of tribal elders and storytellers.

Through the spoken word and repetition, young people learned how to act correctly within their communities and with outsiders. They learned to be quiet and exhibit proper behavior, especially when elders spoke. Through these teachings, Palouse people learn about cultural beliefs, food acquisition and preparation, sources and use of medicines, hunting techniques, gathering schedules, fishing methods, fighting strategies, and a host of other subjects. Young people learned to listen carefully. Their lives and their communities depend on it.

In the presence of tribal elders we have listened quietly and learned. We never took the people or their knowledge for granted. When we interviewed elders, we became their students. We learned from them, and we were richly rewarded. Palouse elders shared knowledge through their memories, experiences, and wisdom that they shared through the spoken word. They often told us of their personal lives, family histories, and relationships with other people. They told us about friends and enemies, joys and sorrows. They indicated where we would find former villages, trails, sacred sites, power places, battlefields, and, of course, hunting, fishing, and gathering places. They told us their family genealogies and explained their relationships with past generations, including notable leaders of past centuries. They explained what they believed made a place sacred. They shared their views on many topics, including historical events, treaties, schools, reservations, and economic change over time. Palouse people pointed out where historical events occurred at the beginning of time as well as during the eighteenth, nineteenth, and twentieth centuries.

Elders illustrated their accounts by telling traditional Coyote stories or legends such as how jealous mountains defaced *Laliik* (Rattlesnake Mountain). They explained where and how they gathered and cooked roots and where they hunted. They told of members of their families who had met explorers, soldiers, agents, ministers, surveyors, road builders. Elders carefully told us cultural and spiritual knowledge, which they felt was appropriate to share. They trusted us with intimate information and counted on us to represent them accurately. Sometimes they took us to places of cultural significance in the heart of Palouse Country. Palouse elders and Indigenous scholars honored us with their knowledge. We have reciprocated by seeking to accurately represent the people and their knowledge; we shared with tribal elders and their families our manuscripts before publication. We have often shared with these families copies of photographs, maps, documents, and the books we have published.

We are indebted to many people and repositories that made *First in This Land* possible, particularly tribal people who have been our teachers. We thank Mary Jim, Carrie Jim Schuster, Andrew George, Emily Peone, Lucy Covington, Gordon Fisher, Wilson Wewah, Suzie Weaskus, Michael O. Finley, Virginia Beavert, Malissa Minthorn,

Bobbie Conner, Antone Minthorn, Ione Jones, David Wolf, Jeremy Wolf, Althea Huesties-Wolf, Ron Pond, and Josiah Pinkham. Others have also been valuable resources including Randall Melton, John Clement, Bruce Rigsby, Brian Carpenter and Paul Sutherland of the American Philosophical Society, Rob McCoy and Trevor Bond of Washington State University, Robert Ruby, John Brown, Ethan Gauthier, and Rodney Frey. Several institutions provided important documents including the Tamástslikt Institute on the Umatilla Reservation, Costo Library of the University of California, Riverside, American Philosophical Society in Philadelphia, and the Franklin County Historical Museum in Pasco, Washington.

We are grateful to our families for their continued support of our time spent traveling, researching, and writing. Clifford would like to thank Lee Ann, Tess, Hayley, and Tara. Richard thanks Lois, Mary and Charles, Karl and Sara, and Leigh Anna.

Clifford E. Trafzer
University of California, Riverside
Palm Desert Campus

Richard D. Scheuerman
Richland, Washington
October 2024

INTRODUCTION

Spreading from the Cascade Mountains east to the Bitterroot and Blue Mountains is the great Columbia Plain. Like a blood line running through the heart of the Plateau is *Nch'i-Wána*—the "Big River" (Columbia). Ancient Indigenous stories explain how *Spilyaí*—Coyote—made the Columbia River waters flow, much to the delight of the plant, place, and animal "People," the first beings on earth. Before the coming of native peoples, these actors put the world into motion in accordance with the Creator's design. Oral accounts have kept alive stories of how these first elements on earth and in the heavens labored to make the world ready for human beings.

By the time the first tribal people arrived, five volcanoes, wives of the Sun, had risen to great heights and the Creator had brought forth Fox, Otter, Deer, Elk, Beaver, Bear, Buffalo, and a host of other animals. Creator assigned Coyote the role of gardener. He planted roots, berries, and trees—all the plants original to the Plateau. Before the arrival of humans, a great flood created unique landforms across the Columbia Plateau, and animal, plant, and place characters as well as spirit beings made ready for the coming of Native Americans.

The *Naxiyamtáma* or Snake River-Palouse were among the earliest Indigenous peoples to build homes along the lower Snake. Their oral tradition tells that the Creator had placed people here to establish villages on the north and south banks of the beautiful stream that sang to the people each day and night. All along the lower Snake River, Palouse men and women built permanent, comfortable, A-framed homes made from logs, lashings, and woven mats. When traveling to hunt, fish, and gather, their horses pulled travois to carry supplies and goods for trading. These travelers used the travois' long poles to set up tipis until they returned home again to their permanent lodges. Palouse villages extended roughly from present-day Lewiston, Idaho and Clarkston, Washington, west to Pasco, Washington.

Tribal people had many friends and relatives throughout the Plateau, Puget Sound, Pacific Coast, and Rocky Mountains. They had strong relationships with Sahaptin-, Chinookan-, and Salish-speakers. Palouse people intermarried with Wanapum, Wallula, Wenatchi, Wishram, Walla Walla, Umatilla, Nez Perce, Cayuse, Yakama, Sincayuse, Spokane, and others. Their paths crossed often through travel across the Plateau in seasonal rounds to gather roots and berries, to fish for salmon, and to hunt for game. These patterns then brought them home along the rivers to spend winters telling stories and preparing for the year ahead.

The Snake River-Palouse and their neighbors were guided by a powerful spiritual belief system they called *Washani*, the relationship of tribal people with their Creator who had made life possible on the plateau, plains, and mountains. Through the Creator's spiritual agents on earth, such as Coyote, life was in balance and sustenance was plentiful for the people. They worshiped—and continue today to worship—in praise and gratitude for the gifts in their environment: fish, game, roots, berries, and plants that gave them food, baskets, clothing, tools, homes, and weapons. *Washani* was of the land and the land enriched their beliefs. The people gave thanks for all things, in prayer and song to their Creator for the gifts of life. Each day prayer warriors would sing to the Creator as a new day dawned.

The spirit world provided important guidance to individuals in different ways. After boys and girls celebrated their tenth or eleventh birthdays, their families took them to secluded places to seek personal visions and spiritual helpers. In remote places, alone, children often received a *wyakin*, a spirit guide, which gave them focus to be great artists, fishers, hunters, warriors, healers, holy persons, leaders, speakers, or ceremonial chiefs. After finding their *wyakin*, children often met with elders who helped interpret the meaning of interactions with the spirit world. These encounters and lessons helped guide their entire lives.

These generational, essential, cultural traditions were challenged with the increasingly alarming arrival of non-native explorers, settlers, soldiers, missionaries, ranchers, farmers, and town builders. Rapid, relentless changes all around them included the introduction of devastating bacteria and viruses. When settlers established governments and began dictating new laws and Indian policies, tribal members grew desperately concerned about their future and the loss of their homelands. To seek guidance from the spirit world, a Wanapum leader named Smohalla from the Wallula area along the Columbia traveled to the slopes of *Laliik* (Rattlesnake Mountain). He returned from his spirit quest with new songs, a dance, and ceremony. The *Washat*, a term derived from the Sahaptin word for "dance," blended with the old *Washani* faith and emphasized that Indigenous people should continue to practice their own faith and remain separate from settler communities. Smohalla and other Plateau religious leaders formalized their beliefs and many Indigenous people, including the Palouse, followed the teachings of the Wanapum prophet. In his own words, Smohalla explained:

> My young men shall never work, men who work cannot dream; and wisdom comes to us in dreams. You ask me to plow the ground. Shall I take a knife and tear my mother's breast? Then when I die she will not take me to her bosom to rest. You ask me to dig for stone. Shall I dig under her skin for her bones? Then when I die I cannot enter her body to be born again. You ask me to cut grass and make hay and sell it and be rich like white men. But how dare I cut off my mother's hair.

Like all their tribal neighbors, the Palouse experienced dramatic changes to their lives and cultures, which resulted from the arrival of

Suyapo, white people. The tribes' seers had envisioned a day when new-comers would arrive, people who would straighten the curving places of nature. During the eighteenth century, they had learned of these newcomers from friends and relatives living along the Pacific Coast. Prophets created songs to use when they arrived. The *Suyapo* brought material culture the Indigenous people had never seen, including pots, pans, metal knives, tomahawks, bells, beads, needles, and a host of other items. They also brought deadly pathogens the Indigenous people had never experienced.

In the fall of 1804, Meriwether Lewis and William Clark led the Corps of Discovery's forty-plus members right through the Plateau, traveling the length of the lower Snake by pirogue past numerous Palouse villages to camp for three days at *Kwásis* ("at the point"), where the Snake River meets the Columbia River in present-day Pasco, Washington. At one large Palouse village, Indigenous people sang prayers and other songs long into the night.

The arrival of Lewis and Clark opened a new era for the Palouse and their neighbors, an era of rapid and destructive cultural change. Today, we know a good deal about the transition from the Native American West to the Settler West. We know historical details through writings of fur trappers, traders, missionaries, soldiers, and settlers. We also have writings of pioneers documenting the hard-won development of ranching, farming, and commerce. These one-sided accounts cast the whole endeavor as victories of civilization over savagery. Written histories glorified and affirmed the winning of the West, rarely turning the lens on the price paid by Native Americans.

Written accounts by non-native people were far less common. Perhaps Nez Perce War Chief Hemene Moxmox (Yellow Wolf) said it best through his oral history of the Nez Perce War of 1877. In his book with L. V. McWhorter, Yellow Wolf concluded, "This is all for me to tell of the war and its after hardships. The story will be for the people who come after us. For them to see, to know what was done here. Reasons for the war, never told. Nobody to help us tell our side—the whites told only one side. Told it to please themselves."[1]

Resettlement of the Native American West changed Indigenous people forever, including the Palouse and every Native American living on the Plateau. However, the settler invasion did not destroy the first people or obliterate every element of their culture, though that was the goal of many non-Indians, including policy makers and educators. In 1892 at the National Conference of Charities and Corrections, Richard Henry Pratt, Superintendent of the Carlisle Indian Industrial School, proclaimed that the United States government had established Indian boarding schools to "Kill the Indian in him, and save the man." The American plan for all-Indian schools was to destroy Native American cultures, languages, and communities while assimilating Indian children.

Though it had many harmful impacts then and into the future, the plan failed. Despite the cultural genocide attempted by the United States government, Native American customs and oral traditions survived. The Palouse and their neighbors survived, preserving important elements of their cultures that are alive today, quietly growing and developing in new ways. Even during the 1970s when Scheuerman and Trafzer began their research, some scholars asserted that the Palouse Indians were extinct. But Palouse elder Carrie Jim countered, "They think we're extinct, but we're not. We are still here." The Jims, along with other Palouse families, are very much alive.

Ancestors of contemporary Palouse people preserved their families, cultures, histories, art, spiritual beliefs, and relationships with each other through the ancient art of oral tradition, allowing their deep-seated attachment to the land, rivers, plants, and animals to continue to exist today. Since time immemorial tribal elders have taught their culture and history and today parents and grandparents, aunties and uncles teach their young people these same lessons. It is the foundation of the resiliency of these peoples.

Documents, discussions, and collections in academic repositories like the National Archives, Library of Congress, or university libraries can only brush the surface of these bone deep memories and stories that shape and imbue the culture. The voices found in this book share a glimpse of tribal truths that have been handed down orally, taught to young people again and again. We are honored to share Indigenous knowledge through the oral testimony of tribal scholars, tribal elders, past and present, in keeping with the oldest literature form known to mankind: oral literature.

Included is the insightful and informative poetry of Palouse elder David Wolf who recently took the name of his relative, Palouse Chief Tilcoax. The book also includes artistic renderings by Palouse illustrator Jeremy Wolf, son of David Wolf, who recently changed his name during a formal ceremony in a Umatilla Reservation Longhouse. Jeremy took the name of his ancestor, Chief Xalish Washumki (Wolf Necklace), son of Tilcoax.

The work also includes the words of Palouse elder Carrie Jim Schuster, the daughter of Mary Jim and Alex Chapman. Carrie grew up with her mother, uncle, and sister in a canvas lodge on the southern banks of the Snake River. For the most part, Carrie grew up in the old way as the family lived off the land, fishing, hunting, and gathering. Carrie offers details about Palouse knowledge including beliefs about the sun and moon as well as days and months. An accomplished artist and educator, Carrie is also a rare speaker of different dialects of Sahaptin, including the Palouse language. Through the oral tradition, she has consulted with and taught us for the past forty years. She and her mother were instrumental in the research found in our book, *The Snake-River Palouse and the Invasion of the Inland Pacific Northwest*.

Roberta "Bobbie" Conner, a tribal citizen of the Confederated Tribes of the Umatilla Reservation and Director of the Tamástslikt Institute, shares her knowledge and that of her family's about traditional ways of hunting buffalo and selectively breeding horses. Brought by the Spanish in the 1500s, horses eventually made their way into the

Native American universe and adapted well to the northern Plains and Plateau, where they flourished on the bunch grass. The Palouse and other tribal people received noteworthy credit for breeding high quality Cayuse and Palouse horses. The small but smart, hardy and loyal animals were prized by many and Indian men, women, and children became renowned as expert riders.

In 1930 Gilbert Minthorn of the Umatilla Reservation recorded several oral narratives, including "*Yamástas*" or Elk Mountain. This marvelous account focuses on Steptoe Butte located in eastern Washington, south of Spokane. *Yamástas* remains a towering geographic anchor for travelers and residents in the region. Many years ago, Gilbert's wife, Atilapum Minthorn, related three important oral stories that had been transcribed and kept protected until recently, and we are proud to publish them with permission, for the first time. Her work demonstrates the significant role of the animals in making the world ready for the first people. Her stories inspired the title of our book, declaring that the Palouse, the *Naxiyamtáma* of the lower Snake, along with other American Indian people, were the "first in this land."

Another Columbia Plateau elder, Samson Tulee offers a detailed description of camping, home sites, and fishing sites on the Yakama River. He details many important places on the Plateau from the Yakama Reservation east to Richland and Pasco. He provides a marvelous description of a rabbit drive as well as excellent fishing areas where the people caught, cleaned, and dried salmon, steelhead, and trout.

Part II centers on the significance of oral histories when conducting community-based research. The work features two *Naxiyamtáma* tribal elders, including Andrew George and Mary Jim. They generously gave of themselves and their time to share many elements of personal and tribal histories. Mary and Andrew grew up on the banks of the Snake but in different villages. They both emphasize the spiritual nature of life among their people and the importance of the ancient oral stories they heard over and over until they could easily repeat them.

7

They speak of two creations. The first includes interactions of characters like Coyote, Salmon, and the Wind, who established the world and the rules by which the people would live. They taught *tamánwit*, lessons to illustrate correct behavior within the culture, laws that guided the lives of the people. The second creation involves the arrival of human beings, their interactions with each other and with the earth, animals, plants, and places. Andrew and Mary also speak of the great changes they saw unfold in their lives in the late 1800s and early 1900s due to the resettlement of their homelands, including the forced removal from their villages.

The voices of the people presented in this work have meaning to individuals, families, communities, and citizens of tribal nations. They have meaning to historians and other scholars, students of tribal elders, and reservation scholars. They have meaning to the world. We write here in the oral tradition, sharing carefully gathered spoken words of a few men and women. The words gift us with knowledge and wisdom of a different time in a special place. These words are as significant today as they were in the past. The knowledge they share in this work will gain new life in the mind and heart of each reader, especially young people seeking to know of the Indigenous past. These words have meaning for the present and future generations who will learn through the oral tradition.

NOTES

[1] L.V. McWhorter, *Yellow Wolf: His Own Story* (Caldwell, ID.: The Caxton Printers), 291

PART I

VOICES AND VERSE

Lee Moorhouse, Thorn Hollow near Mission, Oregon
Wolf Family Encampment at *Leelachpa*, "Many Pine Trees" (c. 1910)

1

GILBERT MINTHORN

YAMÁSTAS—ELK MOUNTAIN
(STEPTOE BUTTE)

Gilbert Minthorn (c. 1900)
Tamástslikt Cultural Institute, Mission, Oregon

Umatilla elder Gilbert Minthorn (c. 1870-1943) was one of several tribal historians interviewed on the Umatilla Indian Reservation in the summer of 1930 by anthropologist Morris Swadesh (1908-1967). Swadesh worked during the summer under the direction of Melville Jacobs (1902-1971) as part of graduate studies in linguistics at the University of Chicago. Jacobs was an American anthropologist known for his extensive fieldwork on cultures of the Pacific Northwest. After studying with Franz Boas (1858-1942), he became a member of the faculty of the University of Washington in 1928 and remained there for the rest of his life.

Morris Swadesh was born in Holyoke, Massachusetts, to Jewish immigrant parents from Bessarabia in southeastern Europe and grew up with Yiddish, some Russian, and English as his first languages. Swadesh earned degrees from the University of Chicago, where he studied with linguist Edward Sapir (1884-1939) and later followed Sapir to Yale University, where he earned his Ph.D. in 1933. The following account by Gilbert Minthorn is in the Franz Boas Collection of American Indian Linguistics (MS 497.3.B63c) at the American Philosophical Society in Philadelphia.

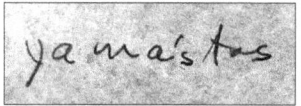

Swadish–Minthorn "Notebook A" Title Page (1930)
American Philosophical Society Archives, Philadelphia

minway'á hiut'se'ya qáqáwa pátamaluwiya. . . . [1]

This is how it was at that [ancient] time.

      He decided and this ground was covered all over [with] water for five years.

            One island named Mt. Yamástas [was] over there.

            No Indians named it.

                [The Creator] held it right there.

Way back before my people, old story. . . .

      Coyote he was smart,

         he knew everything,

In the ground he started to burn fire.
And everybody in the country learn[ed],
    were a witness.
In that time [Coyote] learned everything.
Eat just the same and then fire in that way
    he found fire and made everybody.
He knew us,
    my ancestors
        . . . all of them and right here on the ground.
Everybody learned and the people grew after that.
All of them he finished that one this body [at] that time
    and that was the way he helped
        and that one used to be.
And that time came [the] big ocean all over.
    God [was] his name....

Animal and salmon and fruit and all of the roots.[2]
God named it and that one he knew him,
    all of them he name[d] it.

That time [was] before [the] time [that] White men came.
[The] same way Indians found it out six nights
     and that way working day and one day,
        [a] holy day and that way God and that way God
          name[d] it. . . .
That one [day] nobody do[es] that way.
God's law [tamáluwit][3] [is] that way [for] us,
     all of them that way we know that way in this world.
That [is] the way I know it used to be. . . .

Columbia Plateau *k'pit–limá sápk'ukt* (beaded bag)
Private Collection

NOTES

[1] Minthorn spoke to Swadesh in the Nez Perce Sahaptin language while Atilapum related her oral histories in Snake River-Palouse. Both text series are substantially continuous. Versification formatting here and in other publications is more consistent with Columbia Plateau storytelling traditions and is guided by the excellent work of Rodney Frey, University of Idaho professor of American Indian studies and anthropology, and Carrie Jim Schuster.

[2] Minthorn lists here the elements of the traditional Columbia Plateau First Foods Feast in which participants first share life-giving water followed by the "chief" sustaining sacred resources: salmon to represent fish and venison for animals, followed by plants (bitterroot, camas) and fruits (currants, berries).

[3] "Law" here in Nez Perce is *tamáluwit*; the related term in Snake River-Palouse Sahaptin is *tamánwit*. Snake River-Palouse elder Carrie Jim Schuster explains, "Human beings are to be stewards or proprietors of creation. Humanity exists in *ahtow'* (covenant relationship, sacred trust) with the Creator through which sustenance is provided to people, animals, and plants. This is what Chief Kamiakin and Columbia Plateau leaders of the nineteenth century meant when they spoke to government officials about the 'law' (*támanwit*)."

2

ATILAPUM MINTHORN

FIRST IN THIS LAND

The following three stories were related in 1930 by Palouse-Wallula elder Atilapum (1867-1938), wife of Gilbert Minthorn (c. 1870-1943), and translated by Cy (Sife) Johnley (Walla Walla-Palouse, b. 1907) for anthropologist Melville Jacobs (1902-1971) at Cayuse, Oregon, on the Umatilla Indian Reservation. Jacobs also credited Atilapum's son, Wade Minthorn (1897-1957), for helpful grammatical notes. The original files are in the Melville Jacobs Collection (UW 81/73) at the University of Washington Suzzallo Library Archives. We thank archivist Marc Lindsey for permission to reprint these stories which we transcribed.

How Coyote Made the River Flow

In olden times,
    in the beginning,
        were the people.
The One Who Plans,[1]
    He looked on this land.[2]

He put bodies upon the people,
  the right hand with his right hand,
   and put his spirit inside for thinking.
He put our bodies here in this land,
  and everything across the west toward the
  sunset;
   on the left-hand side there his thought and
   spirit put inside.
He let them go where the sun sets.
We were first in this land
  and then the last ones on the left hand,
   on the sunset side.

The birds and everything in this land,
  ordained with the wind.
The wind cleaned it up
and altogether different birds came here then,
   the same ones everything from then on.
That is the same way deer[3] and creatures
  were all different from then on.
But the first ones,
  the wind cleaned them up,
   that same way.
Instead fire came down,
  water came down, behind it was fire,
   rain first, and there it was water.
The ones that belong here, all over;
  it cleaned them up.

But all the birds,
  they went on through and finished
   the first law.[4]
The same ones were all the birds;
  different then from now.
The fire went out,

Altogether different birds . . . and different creatures.

the fire nowhere in every river, just land.
He also found Coyote,
 far away and alive.
He was there.
"Now I'll go in every land;
 there's no water,
  no water was there.
   I'll be going."

He went far off where water first comes out.
Frog's[5] house was standing there.
Her house was holding back the water;
 She was sitting on the water.
Coyote went after her,
 then he made a law for the people,
  but there was no water and he went far away.
He went and found the house.
"She's holding it back."
Coyote got to her, he went in.
She was sitting there,
 Frog was sitting there
  with water in a small basket.[6]

He said to her,
 "I'm thirsty, Grandmother."
She didn't reply,
 so he spoke to her again.
But she didn't say anything at all.
He asked five times,
 then she gave him water.
Coyote drank from the small basket,
 he swallowed what she gave him.
She filled it with water again.
He looked at it,
 "Oh, water again; give me more water."
She gave it to him,
 then in one gulp he swallowed the water
  from the small basket.

She recognized him now, a Dangerous Being.[7]
 "He has come to me."
She feared Coyote, "A Dangerous Being has come to me."
"Grandmother, now I'll take you away."

He's lying now;
   he planned it.
Now he heard the noise, warriors.
She sat there, she knew.
"Yes, now me; he's holding me to kill later on."
She feared him.
   Oh, Grandmother!
Now he took her by the hand.
"Grandmother, now I'll take
   you home."
He got her by the hand,
   he pulled the earth and all;
   he pulled it out
   and so
   much water.
She tried to
   pull back.
He pulled out,
   Coyote lifted and
   a little more water
   came out.
He pulled against the door,
   and lots of water came out.
He pushed her out of the house;
   the water then started flowing,
    he pushed her behind the water.
"Now you will be just a frog,
   and if the water flows bigger and faster,
    then you will croak, *wá·x̣-wá·x̣-wá·x̣*."

You will be only a frog.
"There are many people,
and why should they be thirsty?
Why should you hold it back?"

**Frog was sitting there with
water in a small basket.**

Then Coyote came,
 he planned this river,
  and the water went far on to the ocean.
And when it got to the ocean
 then salmon[8] came upriver,
  and fish of every kind.

Then salmon came upriver, and fish of every kind.

Young Coyote, Green Cricket, and Old Lady Spider[1]

A chief was living;
 he was the son of Coyote.
His father thought it over,
 "Now I will send him away,
  far away."
   His own son.

He made up his mind,
    and put a pole far up on a tree.
He placed a nest of young eagles[2] up there,
    and said to his son,
        "I have found good birds,
            Eagle's young ones.
                Let's go now, I'll show you."

So Young Coyote went with him.
They saw the birds, nice feathers,
        Eagle's young ones.
Coyote told his son,
    "Take off your shirt and leggings,
        leave them here,
            and the dentalium tied around your hair;"
                That is how you can ascend."

So he climbed
    there up the tree.
He went close to the young eagles,
    but thought, "No, I'll get to them pretty
    quick."

He ascended the pole faraway,
    and got lost,
        up there,
            in the blue sky.
Young Coyote was lost.

Coyote then went home,
    to his son's family
        in this land.
One was named Green Cricket,
    and the other woman was Duck.
        Young Coyote had two wives,
            but now he was lost,
                and they were down here
                in this land.

Green Cricket's child was a boy;
    she had just one child,
        and Duck had none.
Young Coyote was lost for a long time,
    and finally found some people.
They were there afar off.
He found them,
    two old Spider Women.
He went inside their house and told them,
    "I am poor, I am lost, I am hungry."
They said, "You are far away from home,
    and have arrived up here, in the sky."
They made food for him.
    He ate.

One Old Lady Spider told him,
    "You'll have to make a rope."[3]
"Where can I get rope?" he asked.
So they showed him the rope.

He placed a nest of young eagles up there.

They gave him a knife;
    he cut the rope plant like this,
        and he packed five bundles.
He took it back to their house.
They were all glad about the rope.
Old Lady Spider said,
    "Now I'll let you down below."

27

She was fierce, brave, and powerful.
She tied the rope around him,
    then went outside
        and opened up a place
            where she let him down.
He paid with the rope.[4]
He finally stepped down
    and loosened himself.
He shook and pulled at the rope.
She thought,
    "He has surely now gotten down to earth,
        and is sending the rope back to me."
So she pulled it up.

Young Coyote was very glad.
    He went to where his place was,
        and arrived at his house.
Nothing. No people there.
    They must have moved away.
His people and all his belongings were gone.
Nothing was there.
He looked around.
"Where did they go?"
He found a road eastwards they had gone,
    and he followed that.
He got to an old fireplace,
    and continued on.
Then he found the same thing.
Again he went on
    and found a fresh, newer fireplace.
Again he went on
    and found a new one.
        Oh, the fireplace was hot!
"Not very long ago
    they must have just gone."

So he followed them
    and then saw one woman packing on foot.
A child was riding on the pack.
He had found his woman, Green Cricket,
    his wife and baby.
As she went she cried.
He knew her, all of them, faraway.
They had left her behind all alone,
    poor woman.
He pulled back on her rawhide packing rope;[5]
    she didn't see him.
He kept it up, pulling harder to hold her back.
The she saw him.
Oh, she knew, recognized her man!

She sat right down, and told him the story.
"I was behind all the time, and they left me."
"The Chief[6] took Duck for his wife;
    he's up ahead in the lead,
        and he ran us off,
            and we are far away with different people.
He said to her, "In the evening let's follow them."
So they went on that evening.
Green Cricket told him where they stayed.
Coyote Chief arrived there with Duck
    and they also came there
        to the house.
They were all glad;
    they felt good to see each other.
They stayed overnight.

In the morning someone said,
    "Young Coyote is chief, now that he has
        arrived."
Another heard and sang,

They were all glad; they felt good to see each other.

"Coyote, why do you not pay attention?
    Do you not hear that he has come back,
        and that you lied?"
Duck straight away hit Coyote,
    to the water.
She went into the water
    and flew away.

30

Young Coyote thought it all over,
    he knew everything,
        and told the people the story.
"Father Coyote will travel all over the land
        to different places.
That is how it will now be for him."

How Coyote and the Foxes Tricked Each Other

Coyote lay down and went to sleep.
They smelled it from afar.
The Wolf Brothers,[1]
    there were five of them,
        and also five Foxes.[2]
They had been gathering eggs at át'cwatam,[3]
    and cooking them.
They were roasting them in the ground
    and smelled Coyote's salmon.

They ran over there;
    it was still smoking on top of the knoll.
They slowly went over to Coyote
    and took his roast.
Meanwhile he was sleeping.
Aha, they ate it all up, five, ten, fifteen,
    and left the bones piled by the fire.
The Wolves went over to Coyote
    where he was asleep.

With unwashed hands
    they smeared him
        on the mouth
            with salmon grease.
They made his ears pointed
    and his nose and his eyes,
        his narrow eyes.
They fixed Coyote,
    made him a sharp nose,
        sharp ears.
That's what they did to him
    with salmon grease smear.

They left him there
    and went to the lake
        to get the eggs to bake.
They got lots and the Wolves baked their eggs
    and the Foxes theirs.
They baked their eggs in two separate places.
Coyote awakened.
"So I went to sleep after eating too much salmon!
    Only the bones are left.
        I must have eaten everything."
He thought he ate it all up,
    though they stole it.

Coyote went on and on.
"Now I'll be going over there,"
    and he crossed from there to the other side.
He went upriver
    and became very thirsty.
Because of the salmon,
    he went down to the river, and drank.
Then he saw something.
"What is that?"
It was something fearful,
    so he went upriver.
Again he went to drink
    and again it was so.
His eyes were narrow,
    his nose was sharp,
        and his ears were pointed!

He asked his sisters,[4]
    "What has happened to me?
        What is bothering me in the water?
            I am very thirsty but afraid to drink."

Coyote asked his sisters, "What has happened to me?"

33

He was scared from seeing himself in the water.
"Others know it already,
    but you don't.
        The Wolves and the Foxes stole from you;
            they ate up the salmon
                and made your sharp nose
                and narrow eyes and pointed ears,
                and left the fish bones after they had
                    eaten."

Coyote got angry.
"I will track them."
He then ran toward the river
    and drank,
        and drank,
            and drank.
He drank a lot and then pursued them
    far off toward the lake.
He got to a hill and looked down below.
Yes, far off they were indeed baking
    down close to the lake.
"Sleep!" he ordered,
    "All of you, sleep!!"
Then Coyote saw them go to sleep,
    the Wolves and the Foxes.

He uncovered the dirt and leaves,
    and found their steaming food.
He ate the eggs
    leaving five each time;
        one apiece for them.
He put out the fire and closed the pit
    and happily walked away.
When the Wolf Brothers awoke,
    one saw Coyote's tracks and said,

"We tricked a notable person,
            and now we have been paid back."
Coyote continued on his way.
He created places in the river and streams
      where fish could swim so the people could eat
            where they treated Coyote nicely.

"Sleep!" he ordered. "All of you sleep!!"

Atilapum Gravesite
Homli Cemetery near Thorn Hollow, Umatilla Indian Reservation

Many of us have heard the old stories from elders who traveled all across the land and along the rivers and knew their beauty. We can be grateful to our grandparents and others who helped others preserve this heritage through writing and storytelling.

—Alvina Burke-Huestie, Mission, Oregon (2023)

NOTES

How Coyote Made the River Flow

[1] "The one who plans" is *təmyutáin*; "he looked."

[2] "He looked" is from *pátamanwíya*, as if "he ordained / instituted it."

[3] *iwínat* is collectively both deer and elk.

[4] "Law" is *tamánwit*.

[5] *aluq'át*, in this story as animal without a personifying suffix (*-áy, -yái, -ya, -á·ya*).

[6] *taxsmí* is a hard coiled basket, as from cedar root.

[7] From *kw'alalí*, Dangerous Being in myth.

[8] *núsux*, salmon in general.

Young Coyote, Green Cricket, and Old Lady Spider

[1] *Spilyáy, Silksí lkya,* and *Waxalxalí*; Duck is *Yuxyúxya*. Jacobs and Johnley render Coyote in Wallula-Palouse (*Walu'la-Palu·'s*) as *Spilyáy* in this account and as *Spilya'i* in Jacobs' *A Sketch of Northern Sahaptin Grammar* (University of Washington Publications in Anthropology 4:2 [March 1931]).

[2] From *xwayamá*, young golden eagles.

[3] A rope of *taxús*, Indian hemp (*Apocynum cannabinum*).

[4] That is, by letting them keep the rope.

[5] *wátisaspa*

[6] That is, the elder.

How Coyote and the Foxes Tricked Each Other

[1] *xalí·shyama*

[2] *təlpayáima*

[3] "A lake near Ephrata, Washington," possibly Moses Lake which was known as a popular egg-gathering place because of migratory waterfowl.

[4] Huckleberry Sisters. In many stories, Coyote includes his five Huckleberry Sisters who live in his stomach. When he is in trouble, Coyote calls on his Huckleberry Sisters for advice. After receiving their answers, Coyote normally responds, "Oh, I knew that all along!"

3

SO-KO-MAP-O

DEFENSE OF HOME AND PEOPLE

**"'Jean,' Oldest Member of Chief Joseph's Band
Colville Indian Reservation, c. 1901"
Edward H. Latham Collection
University of Washington Archives, Seattle**

*The following oral history was recorded by Colville Indian Agent Henry
M. Steele and enclosed in a December 19, 1901 letter to University
of Washington professor of history Edmond Meany. Professor Meany
made several trips to Nespelem while teaching in Seattle in preparation*

for a book on the life of Chief Joseph. Although Meany never completed that study, he and others like Steele conducted numerous unpublished oral histories of Columbia Plateau elders. This poignant selection is from "So-Ko-Map-O ('Old Jean') Oral History," Edmond S. Meany Papers 0106-002, Box 84, Folder 39, Allen Library Special Collections and Archives, University of Washington Archives, Seattle. Elsewhere the name of the 1877 Nez Perce war veteran, an aunt of Chief Joseph, was spelled To-Ko-Map-Po.

My Indian name is So-Ko-Map-O and the name given to me by the white people is Jean. I was born in the territory now embraced in the state of Idaho, about thirty miles from the present site of Asotin,[1] Washington, on a small stream called by my people *A-la-hah*. This stream empties into the Snake River. As near as I am able to remember, I am ninety years old and perhaps more. My father's name was Che-Lu-Wa-Hiah, a full-blooded Nez Perce. My mother's name was So-Ko-Mop-O and she was a full-blooded Walla Walla. I was named after my mother.

I spent my childhood with my parents pursuing all the pleasures and pastimes of Indian life, hunting, fishing, and gathering roots. I love to think of my younger life; it was so happy and gay. When I was about eighteen years old, I was married to my first husband, whose name was Tom-Ya-Neen. He was a Nez Perce brave, handsome and kind. I cannot say how long I lived with him but seven children were the result of our union—five boys and two girls. They are all now dead, and are buried in different parts of Idaho. I hope to visit their graves once more before I die.

My first husband died and after being a widow for four years I married Skoom-Chits-Ka-Neen, a Nez Perce who was wealthy and owned large bands of cattle and horses. The result of this union was two children, one boy and one girl. The girl has long since died and my son is still living at Nespelem, Washington, and is a member of Chief Joseph's

Band. My son's name is In-Mat-Hia-Hia and the only living child out of a family of nine children.

When Joseph and our people concluded to fight for his forefather's birthright, I was anxious to join him but my husband protested against my engaging in hostilities against the whites. Regardless of his entreaties and objections, I joined Alocott[2] and Joseph and went all through the campaign. I left my house and my husband to assist in the struggle caused by the encroachment of the whites. To go into details of this long and bitter fight would take much time and resurrect many unpleasant memories so I will leave the story to someone younger than I.

So–Ko–Map–O on the Colville Indian Reservation (c. 1895)
Colville Confederated Tribes History & Archaeology Office
Nespelem, Washington

During Joseph's march I often wept in sorrow and shed bitter tears in witnessing the wanton murder of so many of my relations and friends. We often hid in the underbrush and willows to screen ourselves from the musketry of the white soldiers. After each engagement the men would come and tell us who had been slain in battle. Sometimes they would bring us the mangled form of one of our braves whose life was slowly ebbing away. We always cared for the wounded as best we could until death claimed its victim. We generally buried the bodies among the rocks and secreted places. We did this so the soldiers would not know how many had been killed.

After the capture and surrender of Joseph, I left and lived with the Sioux Indians. When Joseph returned from Indian Territory, I joined him at Lapwai, Idaho.[3] In the meantime, my husband had died and his bands of horses and cattle with other property had entirely vanished, having been managed by unscrupulous Indians and bad white men. Many years of my life have been filled with sadness. Death has swept away my children and my two husbands and we have suffered great injustice from the government. It has taken away my old home and declines to allow me to spend the few years that I may live in the beautiful country where I was born and spent much of my younger happy life. The bones of my forefathers are resting there. Little mounds mark the resting place of my children and naturally I would like to be laid at rest there myself.

I am now held as a captive and fed as a common prisoner and for what reason I cannot understand. I have nothing to live for, my Indian pride has been crushed out of me and I fully realize my keen humiliation. I am a member of no church, I belong to no creed but think when I die the Great Father beyond the clouds will be kind and just to me. I believe I will meet my husbands and children, also my departed friends, in the happy hunting grounds and what a happy reunion that will be. I bear no malice or hatred toward anyone and feel kindly toward all. I am an aunt of Chief Joseph and I think him a brave, honest, and fearless man who fought against overwhelming odds for the defense of his home and people.

NOTES

[1] Present-day Asotin is a small community four miles located along the western shore of the Snake River four miles south of Clarkston, Washington. It is named for the nearby Nez Perce village *Hásutin* ("Eel Place").

[2] Alocott (Ollocot, Álok'at, c. 1840-1877) was a prominent warrior and younger brother of Chief Joseph who was killed at the Battle of Bear Paw on September 30, 1877.

[3] In 1885 the Nez Perce exiles in Indian Territory (present Oklahoma) were allowed to return to the Pacific Northwest but not to the Wallowa Valley. Some were permitted to reside on the Nez Perce Reservation while others under Joseph and Palouse headman Húsis Kute were relocated to the Colville Indian Reservation where they lived in the vicinity of Nespelem. So-Ko-Map-O first returned to Lapwai and soon after moved to the Colville Reservation.

4

SAMSON TULEE

FISH WEIRS AND RABBIT DRIVES

Yakama leader Sampson Tulee (1886-1957), son of David Tulee and Susan Tanewashe, was arrested and convicted in superior court in 1939 for off-reservation salmon fishing without a license. He claimed defense under the terms of the 1855 Yakama Treaty that specified tribal rights to "take fish at all usual and accustomed places in common with citizens of Washington." The court decision was overturned by the Supreme Court in 1942 in Tulee v. Washington *with the majority opinion delivered by Justice Hugo Black. The verdict was an important ruling that contributed to the landmark 1974 Boldt decision affirming the rights of Indian fishers that had long been opposed by commercial fishermen. The following oral history was recorded at the Yakama Indian Agency in Toppenish, Washington, by anthropologists Al Mohr and Letiticia Sample and is from a collection titled "Yakima Wishram Fieldnotes [1953-1954]" found in the Bruce Rigsby Papers, Fryer Library Archives, University of Queensland, Australia. Minor edits for spelling and fluency.*

At Prosser dam there used to be trees on the north side of the river. People lived there and down below the next bridge. Some people lived there the year around. An old man named Tap'tatpam lived there. The Horn was called *Wanawīsʸ*. Some people lived here in winter. Some driftwood came. People also camped about four or five miles below Prosser where there is a big bluff and large level place. A place about one or two miles below Prosser was called *Halo'tas.*

At Richland was a place called *Tama'xalo.* Here they got silversides in the fall with a trap. When the water was high they took the traps out. The trap went clear across the Yakima River at this point. It was shallow there. They dried silversides at this place and made "sugar salmon."[1] About six miles below Mabton was the place called *Tsiwa'la.* An old man lived there. His name was Antoine. He was part French and part Indian. He was made to move off the reservation. This was the corner of it.

When the reservation was surveyed to make it small the party of surveyors camped at *Tsiwa'la,* saying it was too far to go down to Prosser.[2] They did not tell the Indians they were going to make it the corner of the reservation, but just that they would camp here. The next morning they went south to the top of the ridge and put a steel monument where there is a gap. There is a prominent gap just back of *Tsiwa'la.* From here the surveyors went west—all the way on Bickleton Ridge. They pointed and took shortcuts instead of riding the whole area.

Tsiwa'la is right on the Yakima [River]. There was a large mussel bed just northwest of Mabton. They gathered these and took them to *Tsiwa'la,* which means "mussels," where there were no mosquitoes. At *Tsiwa'la* they baked, cleaned, and dried them. They stayed here as long as it took to take care of the mussels. Sometimes someone might try to stay the winter if they thought they had enough food to get along by themselves. But usually people went to where groups of people wintered. The place the people gathered the mussels to take to *Tsiwa'la* was called *Ša'panatit,* which means where they packed them, carried them off. They carried them in bags made out of weeds. The place was north and a little west of Mabton. It continued for about a quarter or half a mile. The water was very slow—slough like. There were too many mosquitoes here, too. That is why they brought them down to *Tsiwa'la.*

The mussels were cooked as follows: A hole was dug about one and a half feet deep and about three feet wide. Sticks were laid in this, and rocks were put on top. When the fire burned down the hot rocks dropped in the ashes. Wet weeds were put on top of the hot rocks. The mussels had been washed and were not dumped in. They were covered with leaves and then dirt. In a couple hours they were uncovered and washed. Shells and the mussels were strung together and hung up over fire to dry. In winter dried mussels were pounded up and made into gravy or stew. A small family might use a half-dozen mussels for a meal. The mussels were pierced and the string stuck through. They were pounded in a stone mortar.

The place at Richland [Washington] was where the river was shallow. There were tipis and sheds for drying fish here. Some people wintered there when they thought they had enough wood. They left during high water and gathered roots. Camas was a staple food and Indian carrots. They had some Indian corn in the old days but none of the other vegetables. When the water was low again they came back to get bluebacks. Bluebacks and silversides used to go up to Satus. Silversides used to go up to Toppenish Creek. Now steelheads still once in a while go up to Toppenish Creek.

At the entrance of the Yakima [River] into the Columbia was a year-round village called *Kwa'sis*. It means "The Point" and was on the point between the two rivers. At *Kwa'sis* there were Priest Rapids and some Umatilla Indians.[3] The Priest Rapids and Umatillas spoke that Columbia River language. *Ma'mačats* were Yakamas lived around Ft. Simcoe and on Toppenish Creek. Rock Creek people spoke differently. Wyampams spoke pretty nearly the same as Yakama but a little differently. The people lived at *Sk'in* the whole year around and depended on the Yakama here going to get dry fish and bringing them roots. They had wampum for money.

All along Status [Creek] there were people. Beyond the first and second bridge there was a little falls called *Tamčatni'*, which means "like hanging." The falls has been ruined. A trap was used there. Fish coming downstream leaped into a basket and couldn't get out. Trout were dried here. Steelhead were also caught there. . . . The *Wanawīs'and* Richland people used to go on rabbit drives in the country northwest of Richland. They had a special leader and they sang and beat on tin cans leading to a large net—maybe 100 yards long. The net was held up by a series of posts and hooked on top of the posts. Rabbits became entangled in the net and were killed.

. . .The place at *Halo'tas* used to be a ford for horses. Another ford was just east of Granger maybe a mile. The water here was three or four feet high reaching almost to the armpits—almost had to swim, but a person could walk across. In July and August when chokecherries or service berries are getting ripe rattlesnakes hang around these bushes [at *Tsiwa'la*] to eat. This is the time of year they are getting engaged and married and they are pretty mean.

The *tsiwa'la* was pierced with needles made of greasewood, or *sa'xi*, a hardwood with white flowers. The needle was about five inches long and had an eye in it. Then they were strung on strips of bark peeled from *tamsk'aikska'la* ("climbing up to the top"). Got it about 1 ½ inches thick and pull off the bark—it comes off like string. Two or three dozen *tsiwa'la* would be strung together and then several bunches tied together. These are placed on mats on top of a rack built three or four or so feet off the fire so they won't burn, and turned till smoked and dried. The smoking keeps flies from blowing them.

There is a creek over northeast of Richland—some people called it *Tamaltolwala* ("Pulled Them Over") and some call it *Tolapipi'a* ("Step on Clothes on Rock and Drain Water"). At the mouth of this creek is a white rock ten to twelve feet in diameter that is square and smooth like marble on top. The Chinook Wind and the East Wind fought here. East Wind wrestled all three Chinook Brothers and defeated them. And then Chinook defeated East Wind's three brothers. Then the champions fought. East Wind's sister threw water on the rock and they could not stand on it. Chinook's sister threw it and Chinook felled East

Wind. The sister ran away—holes in the ground [are] her footprints. She got away from sly Coyote. The rock has disappeared. You could see it for a long time below the water a couple feet. It must have come out at high water.

There was no weir at *Taptut*—just the falls. There were some set nets used and dip nets at the falls. The mountain above Prosser at the end of the Rattlesnake Mountains is called *Luksai'* which means Otter. Rattlesnake Range is called *Laliik'*. There used to be large white-tailed rabbits around here. They were called *wilalik'*. The black-tailed rabbit came across the Columbia River when it froze completely over and they drove the white-tails out. Several would gang up on a white-tail. If it circled back they got it sure. The black-tailed ones were called *kat'nam twin'walalik'*. There are some little cottontails around; they are called *ai(u)ks'*. There was no use for gophers. They were called *amix'*.

Wanawīš'—Horn Rapids Fishery (1979)
Richard Scheuerman Collection

The site of *Wanawīs'* is near the northernmost bend of the Yakima River downriver from Prosser. The camp was on the north side of the river below the present dam. There was a falls in the river here. There

49

used to be a little more timber, but sometimes the people burned sage-brush because the wood was so far away. A trap was built clear across the river just below the present dam—where you can still see the rocks and rapids. Umatillas sometimes came and camped on the south side of the river.

At Richland there was a sandy bar and gravel in the Yakama where a person could wade across. One could also wade across here at *Wanawīš'*. At *Wanawīš'* they took silversides in the fall. An old man named *Tsi'utsi'u* used to live here. Another old man who lived here was *Hahas'*. *Wana* means water; *wish* was the noise or sound of the water. Hence *Wanawīš*—the noise of water or wishing water. It was one of the main fisheries.

At Richland they put posts out in the water—they stuck way above the water and wrapped them in red willow. Sometimes they would lose the weir in high water. They would have to save the material for the weir or go a long way to get tall willows for another. There was good pasturage for horses at Richland. Taking the highway out of Richland to Prosser the Yakima River takes a bend. In the curve of this bend (just below the highway bridge) was lots of good pasture and was the camp and fishing place. The weirs were made by placing tripods of posts tied together ever so far across the river, and then tying these together with poles [?]. Then wings were made at the ends (both sides of the river) with traps so that the fish could get into them but not out.

The name of the Richland place is *Tamalkalou*. They caught silver-sides here in October and November. The camp was on the northeast side of the river. The last time there was a trap built here was probably forty-five years ago (c. 1908). Umatillas camped on the south side but kept their horses on the north side. They might go on a rabbit drive from here. Sometimes the Umatilla went to *Wanawīš'* and got them to go too. Rabbits were boiled or roasted and dried to eat. When it was time to use they were soaked overnight to get the smoke taste out. Then they might be boiled maybe with roots.

. . .Silversides were roasted on a stick and when about cooked were scraped out of the skin and smashed onto a mat about twenty feet long. The meat was dried on this mat. When it was dry they took the bones out as best they could and pounded the fish in a wooden bucket made of the root of an oak maybe a couple gallons big. They had a long straight stone rounded in cross-section with which to pound and mash. They saved salmon grease (Chinook and steelhead) and put it in wooden buckets. When a bucket got full they threw a hot stone in and it cooked a little. There was some caution about starting a fire while doing this—to not get the rock too hot or splash the grease. They might then sprinkle up to a half-cup of this grease into a big mortar of pounded salmon. Then it was all pounded together. This was then put into bags holding fifty to sixty pounds made out of $k^wiakluk^wiakla$. There were special places to get this plant where it grew tall. The bags were turned over several times a day for a while. The bags were wrapped in dry rye grass and buried in dry ground. They kept for several months. A family might put up a couple hundred pounds this way. They dug it up before the ground was frozen hard. It might be mixed with *sawíth* or *pyaxí* and is called "sugar salmon." They made sugar salmon at and *Wanawīsʹ* and Richland and some at Prosser.

Three families might live together in a long tipi with three to four fires along it. One family would dig roots, another fish, another would hunt and one would get huckleberries. In the tipi each one might be cooking a different meal at each fire.

NOTES

[1] "Sugar salmon evidently the pounded salmon mixed with grease."

[2] The first government survey of Yakama Reservation boundaries, the "Schwartz Survey" (for surveyor George Schwartz), was completed in 1890 but omitted almost half a million acres that the Yakamas understood to be part of the reservation.

[3] According to Tulee, *Kwa'sis* ("At the Point") was located at the confluence at the Yakama and Columbia Rivers. A Snake River-Palouse village by the same name was located several miles downstream at the junction of the Snake and Columbia Rivers.

5

IKE PATRICK

THE STORY OF THE ANIMALS

Longtime longhouse leader and culture carrier Ike Patrick (1900-1981) was a grandson of Snake River-Palouse Chief Wolf Necklace. He was raised on the Umatilla Reservation but traveled widely throughout the region and knew the family's history and ancestral campsites along the rivers and in the mountains. Ike related details of Wolf Necklace's story to us in a 1981 interview that we included in the book Renegade Tribe *(WSU Press, 1986). Ike also shared many Animal Stories that had been passed down by his grandfather and*

other tribal elders including this one in the 1970s as part of an oral history recording series.

He introduced "The Story of the Animals," from the Tamástslikt Library's Oral History Collection (c. 1977), by saying, "This was told to all of us who were here and in different places. It was a common thing for people to know. Even in those days, they would tell us, 'You can be in the mountains and nothing would bother you. That's the animal law, and even today they won't bother you.' They used to tell us that may be because we might be afraid of the dark. . . . The animals lived by that law. That's the way they used to tell us the story of the animals—how one animal tried to defy all the rest of them and be superior to man."

The Story of the Animals

The leader of the animals was Coyote; the head of the council.
    Then the wolf, then the grizzly bear, then the black bear;
        then the cat family—the cougar, the bobcat, the lynx;
        the deer family—the bucks and the elk.

They were all gathered as one.
    They were like people gathered together today.
        You could call it the Animal World.
          They would cause these animals to speak
          like people.

In their way the animals knew
    there were new people comin' into the world.
        They were clothed.
          The people they referred to were Indians.
            We are speaking of the world here,
            this continent.

The animals had a great question on their mind.
    They wanted to find out just how strong this creature
really was.
        They were talking about man—the human being.

And they talked back and forth all evening.
    But some of them said,
        "We were put on this earth and were told not to bother
this new creation."

And there were some who stated,
    "Well, we've got to find out if they live like we do."
        They wanted to know all these things.

Some said, "No, they live different."
    "Then why is it that we have to leave them alone?"
        "*That is the law*," they said.
          "That is the law."

The law was given to the animals.
    They were given the law of all things
        that they should live with their own.

And that is the argument that came up.
    Here the word came in to one of them with the council—
        the mountain lion.
          He said, "I would like to know who is stronger,
            and who is more intelligent.

It went back and forth in this way.
    The fox was in it; Coyote was in it.
        All because of their being smart and more intelligent.
        They brought these things all out.

When it came to strength, that's what they said:
    "We are told to leave this man alone,
        this human being alone,
          because he is more superior than we are."

And the mountain lion spoke up;
 he turned around and said,
  "Well, just in your mind he is stronger.
   He doesn't have any claws like I have for
    front paws;
     he hasn't got any claws on the feet like
      I have on my hind feet;
   and he hasn't got sharp teeth.
    And at times I can use my tail."

And he whipped his tail about.
 And if you've noticed his tail is almost as long as his body.
  And it's big.
   He turned around and said,
    "If I missed I can always wrap my tail
     around his neck
    like a whip or club,
     and I can beat that human being."

"You'll be breaking the law!"
 But he said, "Well, we'll have to see who is stronger,
  who is more superior.
   And I challenge this man."

So they all objected to his statement that he had made.
 And one, the grizzly bear, he got up and told them,
  "Look at me! I'm bigger than all of you.
   And I honor the law that has been laid down to us.
   I will not break that law."

He said, "Even I wouldn't attempt to challenge man."
 But now this one pointed to the cougar, and said,
  "What a foolish attempt. I advise you not to."

Cougar then said, "I'll go against all of your wishes
  just to prove that I can.

There's a camp down there I'm going to tomorrow.
There's a man who sleeps at the back of the tent.
His bed is there and he sleeps alone.
He is the one I'm going to
attack tomorrow."

And they objected, but could not stop him.
So the next day this meeting continued.
They still tried to talk him out of it.

The mountain lion turned around and said,
"When the sun comes up this next day,
if I'm not back you won't have to wait.
I'll be dead.
But I think I'll be here to meet with you,
to show you who's stronger."

It took all day and night to prepare.
All this time the human being, this Indian, didn't know.
It was his custom to lay down his belt and knife.
That night came and he left his knife and belt
on the side,
never thinking what was going to happen.

About midnight the mountain lion pulled up the tent,
and reached underneath.
He pulled up the tent and grabbed the man's head
and pulled him out.

The Indian awoke and knew he was in danger.
When he was outside he had the presence of mind
that he was quiet too.
But they wrestled around,
got scratched,
claws ripped into him.

He got a hold of that lion and clinched his leg,
    reached around and got his knife,
        and stuck it through the mountain lion's heart.
        That was the end of the mountain lion.

When he jumped up,
    the Indian knew he had him.
        The mountain lion jumped up and trotted a
        little while,
            and fell over, dead.

And then he walked in his camp to the fire,
    by the people who were inside,
        and blew on the coals.
        They noticed he was all scratched up.
        The mountain lion was dead.

The council waited till the sun came up.
    Then the coyote said,
        "Well, I think our friend never made it.
        I think he's dead."

6

DAVID WOLF, JR

THE NEW AND THE OLD WITHIN

**Wilson Wewah, David Wolf, and Jeremy Wolf
with Chief Wolf Necklace capote (2024)
Richard Scheuerman Photograph**

*We were first introduced to the vibrant traditional culture of
Snake River-Palouse and Umatilla families on the Umatilla Indian
Reservation on a trip to the Thorn Hollow district in the spring of 1981.*

Friends had invited us to participate in a First Foods ceremony which introduced us to elders Ike Patrick and Clarence Burke. They related to us the story of Snake River-Palouse Chief Tílqawayks (Tilcoax) and his son, Chief Xalish Wáshumki (Wolf Necklace), who led their people during the difficult years of the 1850s Columbia Plateau Indian Wars and their aftermath. Under Wolf Necklace the family's legendary herds that roamed across the lower Snake River were restored despite recurrent challenges during the era of Euro-American settlement. Wolf Necklace substantially disposed of his stock in the 1890s and eventually relocated to the Thorn Hollow area. David Wolf, Jr. is a descendant of Chief Wolf Necklace who resides on the Umatilla Reservation where he has contributed significantly to tribal language, literature, and other cultural programs.

The New and the Old Within (c. 1969)

Go forward,
My people,
Put away the fish-spears,
Beaded buckskins,
The teepees and the fine
    saddle-trappings,
Put them away
With your warclubs and arrows.

Scorn to dance for pennies
At the whiteman's Round-Up;
Join him in the grandstands
Of his trades and professions.

But do not forget....
The willows by the River Rain,

Remember the Blue Mountains,
The the fire of autumn treetops.
Remember the deer's flesh
Fresh from the killing,
And the neigh of Pinto ponies,
Racing through the
　　whispering rye grass.

Go
To the schoolroom,
The fine brick houses,
The Moon.

But wrap yourself
In memories
As a warm, bright-colored
　　blanket,
Against the chill wind
Of Progress.

Silent Passing (1979)

Fifty-one and ten
I never saw him again—

Listless, ever so silent, I go—
Never again to know.

For the first time the pain must show;
Effortlessly comes the Thundering Blow.

With short years gone by—
There comes another silent sigh.

Then comes the pain and the Thundering Blow.

Twas, sixty-seven and ten
That it happened again.

Thus, came the Thundering Blow;
And once again the pain must show.

Yonder o'er the next hill—
'Tis my time to know—

The fate of the—Thundering Blow.

Winter Blossom (c. 2001)

Across the way
 The midday sun glistens
  On soft upturned pink rose petals.

Thoughts of beauty disperse in a transparent haze
 From the cool gentle breeze
  That crosses the surrounding maze.

The sculpted curves of this blossoming flower
 Radiates in warmth as it
  Highlights the minutes of each passing hour.

While the sweet scent
 Of this spring blossom
  Lingers in the Winter's Day.

'Tis always here to stay.
'Tis always here to stay.

7

EDITH McCLOUD

A GREAT LAW

*Edith McCloud (1924-2010) was born and raised on the Umatilla
Indian Reservation and served as a highly regarded Sahaptin language and cultural consultant. Her father was Walla Walla Chief
John Kanine and her mother, Roseline Wilson, was a member of
the Yakama-Palouse Chief Kamiakin family. After her marriage to
Andrew McCloud, Jr., the couple moved to Yelm, Washington, where
the extended family participated in efforts to procure fishing rights for*

the Nisqually tribe that ultimately resulted in the historic 1974 Boldt Decision. The following oral history was recorded on September 26, 1990 by Lawrence Johnson for the Tamástsklikt Cultural Institute.

I was born on January 19, 1924 at Cayuse [Oregon] to Chief John Kanini and Rosealine Wilson Kanini. We lived in Cayuse until we were ready to start school and then moved to Adams. Choweesapum,[1] my mother's mother, was the most important person in my life, and I think the best woman who ever lived on this earth. She was wonderful. My mother's name and mine sounded Nez Perce, but they're Palouse. The Palouse tend to speak more of the Nez Perce style. My grandfather, his parents are both buried at *Palus* [on the Snake River]. And my grandmother's people were Palouse, my maternal grandmother. But my [paternal] grandfather's family was Walla Walla.

We stayed at home with Choweesapum while our parents went out to pick potatoes, pick cherries, pick whatever there was after the money system came into our lives. We'd stay at home with Grandma while our parents went out, or they would be down the river drying salmon. If we were too young they were up in the mountains digging the roots. Then when you grew old enough to go and do those things, then you went with your parents and learned that way of life, what kind of foods to gather, how to process them.

My maternal side of the family was very, very important in that way to teach us how to live. My grandfather, although he was a chief, our father's father; we were not allowed to be in his camp. We were not allowed to camp in the same area because my mother was a widow. When her husband died, the widow was not allowed in the father-in-law's camp. We camped all over the time of gathering our food, the roots, early spring. During huckleberry gathering season, during the time they fished in those rivers up there, the Wenaha River, Imnaha, Tucannon; all those rivers.

We used to travel to Horn [Rapids, near Richland, Washington] where the people fished, our people fished, and *all* the Indians fished. There were no boundaries or no tribes or "you don't belong here," and such. We used to travel over there, but we never got to go inside [the longhouse]. We couldn't go inside and we might make too much noise, or do something wrong, so we had to stay outside in the wagons. They'd go in there and they'd trade. We'd bring roots, dried roots and different things from this area and go over there and trade for dried fish and dried eels and whatnot. Then we'd come home. But when we traveled to Celilo, our parents would get their fish. They had scaffolds where anyone that came there needed food could get on the scaffold and fish. As much as they needed. You didn't only fish for your own family, but you fished for trading purposes. There was always a commercial trade for fishing and for roots. You traded back and forth.

I saw this kind of tipi [made] out of tule mats there. Several families lived in a long tent like this. They were all related and had their own section. They could live there for maybe all winter together and never have any problems cause they had respect for each other and maybe there would be three fires. You cooked on a certain fire and you lived only in that section. You never bothered anybody else's things, but you could all live together. We all have the same religion. We have the same foods, we have the same manner of dress, and we have the same living quarters, a long time ago.

My grandmother [was blind but] could still weave. She kept the calendar, that ball of string with the beads and knots and everything.[2] She could tell you whose funeral this was and what year this was. She'd show us that ball. It was like a record. In summertime when you're looking for food from daylight until dark you don't have time to make none of this. But you have to gather the things for what you will be making. And then in the wintertime where there is nothing to do, that's when the bags and hats were made, and the men made their costumes. In those times there was nothing you could do in the wintertime but keep warm and do all of these crafts.

They gathered everything that they needed like bear grass and cedar bark. They needed a certain kind of hemp to do this kind of weaving, to make their own string. So everything was made in the wintertime. Even the food, when you lived in a tipi and out in the cold, you had cellars for your food. This was for so many days or months. You stored a lot of things in Indian trunks, *sheptakhai*, like dried meat, dried salmon, roots, and dried berries, and everything.

All your relatives, the older people, they'd say, "I'm your *katla*," or "I'm your *atla*," depending on what side of the family it is.[3] You didn't just call someone that wasn't related to you "grandmother." We never know, because we only called our relatives. And you never called anyone by their name. That's why a lot of these old names you see on records are foreign, because you never used their names. Everyone was an individual, everyone had their own name, and they received it in a ceremony. They gave away—they still do that today. They give away—you can use only your family's names; you can't just choose any name you want. You only use your family names. Like I have my aunt, and she had *her* aunt's name [Tilawtska'áyn], that would be my great aunt. Then she received the name. When she died, then I received the name.

I was always told that when we were put on this earth that we were given a law, a great law. That's the interpretation from our Indian words. When we first were brought to this earth, the Mother Earth, our creator gave us a great law. He gave us a way to live. He gave us certain foods. He gave us our language. He gave us a manner of dress and he gave us our housing. He gave us a lot of laws that we had to abide by to live the right way, the Indian way. And according to history for the most part most of the people tried to live that way of life. There's going to come a day when our Creator will come and he will purify all of this land. When it gets so bad on earth, he will come and he will purify this earth.

I told you everything He gave us, and then He gave us our ceremonies. There's nothing on this earth that you take or use unless you pay for it. There's not any kind of food that we have or that is our own, like our salmon, our roots, our berries, and whatnot, that we don't have a feast for before we can start using it for our own families. We have to have a feast. And before you have any feast you must always remember the people who have gone on before us, to make the ceremony. And the ceremony is supposed to start on a Saturday. And the main day is Saturday, and then it ends on Monday. Cause that's the way our language is: Saturday means *Waawheet*, means the Beginning. Sunday means *Pachoiwit*, the Day, and then Monday is *Wanait*, the End. And we have to know our language, and we each have to have a native name, our own name. . . .

We never had longhouses a long time ago. We had individual family ceremonies. There'd be maybe ten families in one family, one of those houses. When they were ready to go and get their salmon and have their first salmon, they'd have their feast. It wasn't like you'd invite everybody from around the country. Of course they'd be welcome. And same way with the root gathering. You had your own individual family gathering. That's the way it was a long time ago. Today it's carried over to more of a social function, and you invite everyone to come, which is nice, but that's the way it's carried on today.

This is your body that you borrow while you're here on Mother Earth. The spirit is yours. And when your body dies and you're put into the ground and your head is facing east, your spirit will leave you. But it'll come back together again at that time of purification. That's why you're buried in a certain place and should stay there. But they've been moving all of these different graveyards, picking them up, the skeletons and everything, and moving them, lumping them together. That's wrong according to our people; they're supposed to stay there, wherever they were buried; they're supposed to stay there. This is what the old people tell us, because there's going to come a day when you come together and you have to answer to the Creator. And you have to know your language, and you have to have a name.

We have got to have leaders who want to take care of the children, the unborn children, seven generations down the road. We have to have people like that.

NOTES

¹ Chowesupum's namesake was one of Chief Kamiakin's wives, else-where spelled Chamesupum and Yumasepah, and also known as Mary Kamiakin (c. 1845-1920). She resided in adulthood with other members of the Kamiakin family on the Colville Indian Reservation near Nespelem, Washington.

² A "time ball," or *ititamatpamá*, fashioned with string typically made from Indian hemp or nettle.

³ *katla*: maternal grandmother; *atla*: paternal grandmother.

8

MARJORIE WAHENEKA

THE BOUNTY OF THIS LAND

Marjorie Waheneka (Et-twaii-lish) is a food gatherer for the tribal Longhouse at the Confederated Tribes of the Umatilla Indian Reservation. Her grandfather, McKinley Williams (1892-1968), was born on Penawawa Creek in Snake River-Palouse country and often told his descendants, "Never forget you are Palousepum (Palouse people)!" He shared many stories of tribal history and knew the old

fishing and hunting sites along the Snake and Tucannon Rivers that were shown to him by his father, Victor Williams (Itsayáya-katchna-katchpaína). "I do not know everything and will never say I do," Marjorie explains, "but the traditional knowledge I acquired came from older people who lived during a time when life was hard physically and mentally but who survived to share their knowledge and experience." She was the first Native American ranger at the Whitman Mission National Historic Site, later served as assistant director of the Tamástslikt Cultural Center, and participated in the 2022 Whitman College Long Tent Symposium. The following article was first printed in the Oregon Historical Quarterly *106:3 (Fall 2005).*

I was asked to present the Indian perspective on food and culture. I agreed to the assignment with the intent of "clearing the air," as the saying goes. When I sat and thought about this subject it came to me that, yes! I should be truthful. I have had the opportunity to work on an exhibit at Tamástslikt Cultural Institute on the Treaty of 1855 relating to the Cayuse, Umatilla, and Walla Walla tribes. For two years I researched material. I visited the National Archives in Maryland, where I viewed the actual Treaty papers. I visited the Washington Historical Society in Tacoma, Washington, and examined the Gustav Sohon drawings done at the treaty council. I attended several public programs by Paul McDermott and David Nicandri on Sohon and the Treaty of 1855.

All this research leads me to say that what is described as the "Chiefs at Dinner" drawing is that many interpretations will come forth. In *Northwest Chiefs: Gustave Sohon's Views of the 1855 Stevens Treaty Council*, author David Nicandri presents a copy of the drawing and an explanation underneath. Also in the book *Life of General Isaac I. Stevens*, by Hazard Stevens, a description is given of this dinner. I, too, have read the Treaty proceedings recorded by various individuals, and it was the Nez Perce group that dined with the officers. They were the only tribal group who took the rations offered by the U.S. Army officials.

The Cayuse leader Young Chief spoke up and told Stevens he had his own provisions and was providing them for others like Kamiakin the Yakama leader.

**Gustavus Sohon, *Chiefs at Dinner, Walla Walla Treaty Council* (1855)
Washington State Historical Society**

I have learned much these last few years researching for the exhibit our facility has on the Treaty of 1855. The Confederated Umatilla Tribes is the first Columbia Plateau tribe to work with the National Archives in Maryland to request a loan for pages from the 1855 document. It was expensive and the restrictions overwhelming, but when the documents arrived at our building an overwhelming feeling was felt by the drivers who transported the documents out here and by staff who accepted the delivery. These four pieces of paper out of eleven pages came "home" after being housed in a temperature-controlled building, locked up in a security-tight room where appointments are made in advance to view them. The feelings were of "feeling scared," anxiety, tears, and a heaviness in the heart. Staff immediately gathered in the room with the documents in a special crate and conducted a prayer service to ease the "feelings" and to welcome the papers "home." At the end were three prayer songs, songs the men whose "Xs" mark an agreement to cede lands to the U.S. government sang 150 years ago in the Walla Walla Valley. Those who gathered in the gallery reassured our ancestors who made their mark that we did not forget their sacrifice and their thinking seven generations into the future for us.

I sought advice from the "old men" of our sweathouse, several elders, and both Tribal and Federal co-workers about these matters. I appreciate very much their listening, their insight and advice. I am one of the food gatherers for our Longhouse, a duty I have committed myself to since 1974. An elder aunt asked if I was interested in assuming a role my mother had, since they were both the same age and at the end of the line. My aunt was the head food gatherer, a position I would have to work my way up to. I really didn't have a choice. My grandmother just told my aunt, "Yes, she'll do it!"

**Tamástslikt Librarian Malissa Minthorn Horn with
1855 Walla Walla Council Umatilla Treaty Copy
Tamástslikt Cultural Center**

A longhouse is a community gathering place. Traditionally, our Longhouses were made from bulrush or tule reeds sewn into mats using string made from dogbane. These mats were laid on pole frames measuring anywhere from 50 to 150 feet long. The width depended on who was instructing the group. If it was really cold, dirt would be piled along the bottom of the pole frames to a depth of a foot or more. Both the earth and the tule reeds offered insulation. The mats were laid on the pole frames in layers, and when it would rain or snow the top layers acted like a sponge, soaking up the moisture and swelling up so the rain would run off just like it does on roofs today. Tule lodges were set up during the winter months, and several families lived in each.

At gatherings in the long tule lodge, everyone sat on the ground. Special tule-reed mats were sewn (twisted) to make the "table," and more simple mats were used for rugs. The only protocol for seating was that the male drummers sat at the head of the table and others sat in a semicircle, maybe twice around the edge, depending on the size of the structure and how many people were in attendance.

I used to hear my Grandma say that a long time ago, before community Longhouses were built, private homes were used or a family would build a long tent by placing all their tipis on a long pole to make a frame similar to a tule lodge. The cooking was done outside on camp stoves in great big pots, and the salmon and deer were placed on wooden spits and roasted over the fire. She said sometimes they had to serve two or three times at community meals, clearing the table of dirty dishes, setting up clean ones to serve another group, and repeating the process. We had to heat lots of hot water in big galvanized tubs to do dishes and hang our dishcloths on clothes-line to dry. We used "real"—enamel—dishes and serving dishes, saucers, cups, and utensils. Today we are spoiled because we use paper products when possible. There are some Longhouses where people still hang on to the tradition of using "real" dishes but also have modern dishwashers or plenty of big sinks and space to wash, dry, and store the dishes.

Today many tribal people utilize their Longhouses for dinners no matter what the occasion. A modern Longhouse is a building with one large, open space where "church" services are held on Sundays and funerals and other special ceremonies are conducted, which the tribal community attends. The building also has a separate cooking area with commercial stoves, ovens, kitchen counters, and a dishwasher with big sinks and more counter space. Some have bathrooms with showers and benches like a gym, big storage areas, or separate rooms used for smaller functions like family dinners or fund-raising events.

Food is part of many of our ceremonies. In addition to the first food feasts, there are the first kill and salmon feasts for the boys and first roots and first berries feasts for girls. Food is also important at gatherings that mark weddings, baby trades (when in-laws exchange gifts between the families and for the new baby), funerals, receipt of an Indian name, and the end of a mourning period as well as modern events recognizing birthdays and sport or educational accomplishments. It doesn't have to be anything special, just your family getting together all in one place. When food is shared and eaten, it is a time to open your heart and speak truthfully about how you feel.

What type of foods might be served? There are two answers to this question: 100 to 150 years ago the Indian people survived on the Indian foods provided by Mother Nature. Their diet consisted of salmon and other types of fish available from the nearby rivers and creeks; deer and elk meat; berries; and the roots of bitter root, biscuit root, camas bulb, Indian carrot, and a variety of others. Such roots are now scarce because private landownership, the grazing of animals (cows and sheep), and the use of pesticides block access or interfere with plant growth. Berries included huckleberries, chokecherries, blackberries, wild strawberries, gooseberries, elderberries, and others found along the Indian trails. It was after contact with non-Indians and the establishment of the Hudson's Bay Company in the area that other foods became available. In 1836, when Marcus and Narcissa Whitman established a mission among the Waiilatpu band of Cayuse Indians, Marcus Whitman became the first farmer in the area. Some of the Indians were soon planting their own gardens.

The second answer to this question concerns contemporary times. There has always been a small group, mostly from one family, who have managed to maintain their traditional identity while living the *natitayt tamanwit* (Indian law). This family group still goes out to fish and dry the fish. They hunt and dry or cut up and freeze the meat, and some even bring the meat to a commercial meat-processing business and have it made into burgers, steaks, roasts, and sausages. The women still do the work of the food gatherers—they go out and dig the roots and dry them and pick the berries, which they preserve by canning. All is kept for ceremonies, funerals, and feasts. This small group provides traditional foods for community functions, and they also work in the kitchen to prepare and serve the foods. Today, traditional foods are served along with modern dishes such as salads, fresh vegetables, stews, cakes, pies, fresh seasonal fruits, and whatever any guests contribute to the meal.

The women do most of the cooking, but we change with the times just like anyone else. Today we have men who cook the meat and salmon outdoors on grills, and the rest of the preparation is done in the kitchen by the women. Traditional roots are boiled just like macaroni or rice and eaten plain or with sugar. The Indian people always planned ahead and had their cache, not only with food but also with material things for funerals and ceremonies recognizing naming, first kill, salmon, roots, berries, weddings, baby trades, and memorials. We were always taught to have things available when the need arises. In contemporary times, it is easier and cheaper just to go to the nearest Wal-Mart, Kmart, ShopKo, or Target to purchase inexpensive items. Before, all giveaway items were handmade, with the work done throughout the year. If a person was in good financial status they purchased the better blankets, shawls, and material to sew their own clothing. My Grandma said even horses with all the gear and cows were given away if a person owned them. I recall my grandmother telling me that when people gathered at their home, it was to conduct business or prepare for a special event.

Left: Canned Powdered and Dried Salmon
Right: Canned Chokecherries and Huckleberries

After the meal, the women and children were sent out of the room and the men discussed matters. After decisions were made, the women were invited back in to discuss preparation tasks. My Grandma said it was a joint effort of a married couple and their families to have open communication and respect for one another to accomplish big events. Today when food is shared we are reminded that it not only nourishes our bodies but it also strengthens our bond as family and friends, and so it is medicine for the heart and soul. I was recently reminded of that when a death occurred in our family unexpectedly. So many family and friends came to the funeral, and it was a reminder to our family that we were not alone. The people came to show their support and express their love and respect for our family.

The Indian people were very hospitable folks, as has been recorded by many non-Indian people in diaries, books, and oral histories. I was taught as a child that when company came to your home you offered them something to eat and drink immediately and if you didn't partake of what was offered you offended your hosts. It didn't matter if you had just eaten, you would have to eat again. I can still hear my Grandma say, "Even if you just offer them bread and water, give it to them."

Indian groups have always been a "curiosity" to non-Indian people.

Ever since Lewis and Clark we have been documented for our culture, traditions, language, religion, foods, and lifestyle. Even today the documentation continues by college students working on dissertations. Personally I am thankful for these people as they have done what some of us have thought about but for whatever reason never done! I am thankful to Gustav Sohon for being present to record with an artist's eye and hand interactions among the people at the 1855 Treaty Council. He left behind what he saw—the people, the landscape, the camp scene, the activity, the dress, and various age groups present during that time.

Being a lady of the Longhouse is a big responsibility, one a person can't just do when she feels like it or when it fits into her schedule. You take on the responsibility of being a servant to the people, the community. The responsibilities can overwhelm a person, especially if she wasn't raised by an older person, which is one reason why we try to recruit and train our younger daughters, nieces, and granddaughters.

Traditional Umatilla Longhouse Feast (c. 1960)
Tamástslikt Cultural Center

I learned my duties by observation and by asking questions. I had very patient grandmothers and aunts who taught by being involved, by action, and by example. When my aunt came to ask me to serve as a food gatherer, I had to ask my Grandma, "So what am I supposed to do?" She explained that I was going to be taking care of the foods given to us by the Creator. I would go out and dig the roots, pick the berries, and bring them back for the people in the community to eat at the new foods feast. Foods are gathered in a seasonal round, and after the new foods feast is held the community would be allowed to go out and dig the roots or pick the berries to prepare for the winter months. I would also be at the beck and call of families within the community as a cook or kitchen helper for funerals or other ceremonies conducted at the Longhouse. The most important events I am involved with are the celery feast in March, the root feast in April, the Fourth of July Horse Parade, and the Huckleberry Feast at the end of July or early August.

There has always been a small family group who still practice the traditional ways, and my family has been the strongest on our reservation. There have been times we have been completely exhausted beyond measure. As I get older I find it harder to bounce back. My stamina is weakening. My aunt is no longer able to go out digging or huckleberry picking with us, and so the prayer songs she sang are no longer heard at the beginning of our day. These last two years that responsibility has fallen down to me, because I know songs from our Indian religion and I have also struggled to learn my Indian language—two high requirements for a woman leader. There are several women older than me in my family, but the responsibility has come to me and I didn't refuse. I close my eyes, envision my Grandmas, pray from my heart, and the words and song come before we go out and dig or pick the new foods.

I refer to my grandmother a lot because she was my teacher, and I held her in very high esteem. She was also the oldest daughter of Chief Willie Wocatsie, co-chief of the Walla Wallas and a recognized leader on our reservation. She shared so much oral history with me, and many times today I reflect back on her teachings to keep myself in order. She was born near Bickleton, Washington, in 1902, and when her mother was widowed around 1910 they moved to the reservation of the Confederated Umatilla Tribes. My Grandma made her home and raised her family along the Umatilla River until her death in 1981. I was by her side until she left us behind.

I am forever indebted to all my elders—grandmas, grandpas, parents, uncles, aunts, brothers, sisters, and children for giving me the strength to believe in the Creator and all the bounty of this land; to look into the future with promise, as now I am a teacher and an example to my children, nieces, nephews, and grandchildren; and to preserve and protect our culture and heritage to the best of my knowledge. Thank you all for allowing me this opportunity to express my teachings and the love I have for this *tuicham* (land).

9

BOBBIE CONNER

"GOING TO THE BUFFALO"
BISON AND HORSES

Bobbie Conner
East Oregonian **Photograph**

Roberta "Bobbie" Conner is the Director of Tamástslikt Cultural Institute on the Umatilla Reservation near Pendleton, Oregon, where she works to perpetuate the knowledge and histories of the Cayuse, Umatilla, and Walla Walla people. Bobbie, who was raised on the Umatilla Reservation, spent her early career in Seattle working for the United Indians of All Tribes Foundation. After earning a Master of Arts in Management from Willamette University, and working for thirteen years for the Small Business Administration, she returned to her Oregon home in 1997. She has been working to depict an accurate history of the tribes of the Columbia River Basin.

Bobbie currently serves on the Oregon Historical Society Board of Trustees, the Oregon Community Foundation and the Nixyáawii Community Financial Services Boards of Directors, and the Tamkaliks Celebration Committee. Her past board service includes Wallowa Homeland Project, Oregon Cultural Trust, Eastern Oregon University, National Museum of the American Indian, American Alliance of Museums, National Council of the Lewis and Clark Bicentennial and its Circle of Tribal Advisors, and the Lewis and Clark Bicentennial in Oregon. She has been featured nationally on CBS Sunday Morning and numerous other documentaries. Bobbie provided the following oral history on January 9, 2024 to Jesse Bird, Tamástslikt Institute Education and Interpretive Specialist.

Bison and horses have long been significant to the Columbia Plateau, including the Cayuse, Umatilla, and Walla Walla Tribes of the Confederated Tribes of the Umatilla Reservation where I live. This is also true of the other tribes of the region, including the Palouse, Nez Perce, Wanapum, Wishram, Wenatchi, Spokane, Sincayuse, Sanpoil, Kalispel, Klickitat, Yakama, and others. Contemporary Indigenous people of the Plateau are ancestors of my tribal people who "went to Bison" or "went to Buffalo" for a very long time. There is archaeological evidence that Yellowstone obsidian made its way to the present-day state of Washington as early as the 1300s. Among our tribes, there is considerable oral history about bison hides, which were of great importance and value in trade, wedding ceremonies, and burial rites. We once used buffalo hides as gifts and means of exchange. Bison hides were highly significant in our daily use. Our people used the hides as the lining or as beds inside our tule-mat lodges. Over time while our people were going to Buffalo, they encountered dramatic changes.

At one time, bison lived near to us in present-day Baker and Union Counties in Oregon near the Idaho border. The buffalo that once lived in the Plateau also inhabited the John Day River area. Our people hunted these smaller bison on the plateau as well as traveled to the Buffalo Plains to hunt the larger animals. We have oral histories that talk about these buffalo, and one or more skulls of these smaller species of bison have been unearthed nearby the Umatilla Reservation in Oregon. So, before modern generations there was a time when bison populated this landscape, not in the numbers they were found on the Great Plains, but they were present in this region. The Native people of the Columbia Plateau have a lengthy relationship with bison both in our area as well as in the Yellowstone region east of us.

Before the modern horse came to this continent, people traveled on foot to the buffalo in inter- or intra-tribal parties. The Native people journeying to the Buffalo Country east of us to the Yellowstone River Valley were all able-bodied folks. The trip was long and often difficult. Once the parties arrived on the Buffalo Plains of present-day Idaho, Wyoming, and Montana, they often lived there for two or three years, often over the course of two winters. Usually, it was a couple of the able-bodied young women who traveled with a delegation of men to the Yellowstone area. We are connected to that landscape as well as our own, because the largest tributary of the Columbia River is the Snake River. The 1,078-mile journey confluence from the Snake and Columbia to the headwaters of the Snake takes us to that bison country. Our people traveled the major trails across the Bitterroot Mountains, including the Lolo Trail toward present-day Missoula, Montana, and we knew the Big Hole and other important places from the Columbia River Valley to the Yellowstone River.

When our people went there, they could not carry back a lot of meat, hides, or trade goods because they were on foot. As a result, they might fight enemies like Bannock, Shoshone, and Paiute peoples. In the process of making that trip, they sometimes took enemy captives, using them to carry their burdens home. So, their delegation might grow while away from home. When they returned to the Plateau, they often brought paints, vermilion, from the Yellowstone area. They also obtained obsidian or volcanic glass, which they used for arrow and spear points. They returned home with bison-haired dolls, things they manufactured while living in the Buffalo Country. They returned home with tools made from Bison bones, including horned spoons, sewing awls, scrapers, hoes, knives, arrowheads, lance points, and needles. People returned home wearing coats made of buffalo hides and gloves.

In the early 1700s, our people acquired horses. They could carry far more home from the Yellowstone region, including dried meat, hides, horns, bags, and other trade goods. We had a strong relationship with the vast landscapes of Buffalo Country, and today, at least twenty-six contemporary tribal nations are affiliated with what is now known as Yellowstone National Park.

This history of being buffalo hunters was important to our people in the Treaty Council of 1855. Native leaders explained to the American Indian Superintendents Joel Palmer and Isaac Stevens that Plateau people had a long-term tradition of going to the Buffalo, which could be dangerous due to attacks by Bannock, Shoshone, Paiute, and other tribes. We explained to the treaty commissioners of the United States about these skirmishes and tribulations we had with other tribes. They often made trouble for us as we traveled to and from the Buffalo Country. Other Native people made trouble for us while living and hunting in the Yellowstone area. As a result of these attacks, Plateau people often traveled in multi-tribal groups for protection. As a result of so many people traveling to the Yellowstone region, our people learned many languages, including a common sign language that men, women, and children used during inter-tribal gatherings to trade, visit, and socialize.

The modern horse came to our people from the Buffalo Country. Spanish settlers brought horses to Mexico and the Southwest. The horses made their way north onto the Great Plains and the Rocky Mountains. From there, they came west onto the Plateau where horses thrived during the eighteenth and nineteenth centuries. Not long after the first horses arrived, our people began selectively breeding. We bred for and developed an amazing animal that came to be known as the Cayuse horse. The Cayuse horse or a Cayuse became a slang term for an "Indian pony," or "small horse," or "wild pony." Because of the Cayuse horse, different places throughout the American West became known as Cayuse Junction or Cayuse Pass. They got these names because Cayuse horses gathered or traveled to landscapes far and wide. So, the name "Cayuse" became common in many parts of the West and is reflected in literature, song, and music of the West.

We were the first people to breed the Cayuse horse. Tribal people, including Cayuse, Nez Perce, Palouse, Umatilla, Walla Walla, Yakama, and others bred the Cayuse horse. The name became synonymous with smart, tough, intelligent, and quality horses. The Cayuse horse was a small, not very refined headed horse. My teachings from Indigenous relatives, all of whom were horse people, taught me that all that we cared primarily about breeding sound horses that would serve our people well in many diverse circumstances. Our ancestors cared about the soundness of the horse. Since we did not shoe our horses, we could not have horses with soft or fragile feet. The feet and leg bones of a Cayuse horse had to be hard and strong. So, for our people, hard footedness and straight leggedness and soundness of the feet and the bones were first and foremost.

Our people bred the Cayuse horse for endurance or durability, stamina, came from the heart girth—the lung capacity of the horse. We often would run our horses thirty or forty miles a day and for multiple days in a row. A Cayuse horse had to have stamina because we generally trained our horses to jog, trot, or canter when we moved along. Most often, we did not walk our horses, but when we did, they could cover a lot of ground with their sturdy legs. Because of their short legs, a Cayuse horse is incredibly comfortable riding at a lope or a gallop. A Cayuse horse could travel smartly and capably on talus slopes, rocky hillsides, and steep terrain. Cayuse horses have keen eyesight. They can carefully navigate through heavily forested lands and fallen trees like those found on the Lolo Trail. They are so much better at handling our varied landscapes on the Plateau and mountains than any long-legged or long-backed horses. So, they were bred for where we needed to go and how we needed to travel.

We bred the Cayuse horse for intelligence. For horse breeders, two different types of intelligence exist, including intelligence of the mind and intelligence in movement. Horse riders never want to be on a stupid horse, especially in risky terrain. Riders want to be on a horse that knows how to pick its way around trees and shrubs and rock, particularly in forested steep slopes. You want to be on an intelligent horse when you are wading through difficult waters. We bred Cayuse horses for their athleticism and muscle tone. The movement of a horse is part of what we call intelligence, and the Cayuse horse is highly intelligent in all respects. We bred our horses to be honest so that what we see is what we get. We bred our horse, and still do, to be true to its rider and avoid accidents and injuries to the animal and rider. We bred and trained our horses not to get excited, to be calm under fire and level-headed.

For one hundred years, breeding quality Cayuse horses was our stock-in-trade. Horses were one means of our wealth. In 1805, when Meriwether Lewis, William Clark, and the Corps of Discovery passed through our lands, they commented that the Nez Perce, Palouse, Cayuse, Walla Walla, Yakama, Umatilla, and others were wealthy people with hundreds of horses. Fifty years later, at the time of the Walla Walla Treaty of 1855, Indigenous families on the Columbia Plateau had thousands of horses. Our tribe was the largest livestock-producing tribe per capita in the United States in the 1890s. We had many horses grazing

"Treaty Rock" Commemorating the 1855 Walla Walla Treaty Council
Whitman College Campus; Walla Walla, Washington

on our homelands, but we also grazed thousands of head of cattle. Our country was and remains well suited to grazing livestock.

Cayuse horses were herd-bound, meaning they bonded with each other and remained together on the open Columbian Plains. Before branding, the great horse herds of various Indigenous families stayed together as they moved about to graze and water. Cayuse horses were also bound to their owners, the families that cared for their horses. They were loyal to their people and formed strong relationships with their owners. Thus, the people had a strong relationship with their horses and the horses had a binding relationship with families and individuals within tribal groups. In part, this reciprocal relationship emerged from the close interaction of horses and human through selective breeding. Our people were highly skilled at selective breeding, and this is a significant element of life among the Native people of the Plateau.

For example, my grandfather selectively bred for white horses or albino horses. He traded in matching pairs of white and light-colored horses, because settlers with money to spare wanted matched teams of horses in front of their wagons or surreys. We used horses when we went hunting or fishing. When we traveled our seasonal rounds, going to early root grounds, fishing areas, hunting places, our horses served us as transportation through the yearly seasonal rounds and carried home the roots, berries, fish, and meat we had worked hard to acquire for use throughout the year. We relied on our horses to carry mothers and babies, small children, and elderly people. We bred Cayuse horses to be smart and courageous when they encountered rattlesnakes, bears, cougars, and other predator species nearby. When we hunted bison on the Plains, our Cayuse horses were trained and highly skilled at racing alongside of buffalo so that our hunters to take down the animals with bows, arrows, and lances. The life of our buffalo hunters depended on the ability of their mounts to navigate the movements of the bison. The relationship of the horses with their riders was indispensable for the rider and his horse.

Back in the days of traveling by seasonal round, we relied on our horses. In the early spring, usually in March, our people packed up their horses and traveled to early root gathering grounds. Then we returned to the rivers near our home to fish and dry salmon and eels. Toward fall, we traveled to hunting and berry grounds. As the weather became colder and winter was in the air, we returned home to end that year's round. To begin our seasonal round, the women packed the goods we needed while living on the trail, camping, harvesting, gathering, fishing, hunting, and processing our foods.

My great grandmother's generation lived the old life of a seasonal round in the early twentieth century. She was a young girl at the turn of the twentieth century, and her generation continued the practice of the seasonal rounds. They relied greatly on their horses to accomplish the seasonal round. She traveled with her father, mother, aunts and uncles, and older sister with their dogs on the trials to root grounds, fishing areas, and hunting places. They would leave their home with eight to ten horses, and by the time they came home, they would have twelve to twenty horses in a pack-string carrying their foods, in addition to the horses they originally rode and packed out to begin their seasonal round.

In the early 1900s, my grandmother's family brought home sufficient goods to take care of themselves, share with relatives, host guests during the winter, and to trade for other items. They returned with enough food and medicines to share with members of their community who needed help. They brought home sufficient foods, medicines, materials to make tools, paints, and hides for wedding exchanges, feasts, and ceremonies. Their goods lasted through the winter months until spring when they would prepare and pack their horses for another seasonal round. She lived at a time when her family was bonded to other families in the community. They understood the principle of reciprocity and shared and helped other families within the community, knowing that they might need help one day and their neighbors would be there to help them.

Tribal Roundup Near the Mouth of the Yakima River (c. 1910)
Franklin County Historical Society, Pasco, Washington

When our people traveled on seasonal rounds or rodeo off to the Buffalo Country, they traveled in larger groups, many times upwards to one hundred or more people. They might travel with many horses across the Plateau, into the Blue Mountains, and west into the Cascade Mountains. As they traveled, they were vulnerable to attacks from other Native Americans. This was especially true if they had traveled east coming home up the Snake River. Our last fishing, big fishing, would occur around Weiser or Payette in the mountains of Idaho or along the Snake River. This area was about halfway between Bison Country and the Umatilla Reservation. The people traveled in larger groups to protect themselves and their goods from Bannocks, Shoshone, and Paiute raiders, eager to steal the goods our people had packed to bring home. Our people were continually vulnerable to attacks when we traveled through the edge of the Great Basin and into the Grande Ronde Valley where our great grandmother, who was a medicine woman, was killed in a Bannock raid. Fortunately, her children, my relatives, escaped on horseback on the Black Hawk Trail.

The history in our family with horses goes back to the Wallowa Country. On my grandfather's side are the people from the Wallowa Valley of eastern Oregon who selectively bred Appaloosa, or Palouse horses. The Eagle Cap Wilderness rises dramatically above Joseph, Oregon. That region has incredibly steep terrain with nineteen peaks that rise over 9,000 feet. This gives you an idea of what kind of horses you had to have to operate in that country. The Nez Perce and others living in the Wallowa Valley bred Cayuse and Palouse horses capable of taking riders into the mountains to hunt and gather. They were smart and careful mounts that knew how to weave their way through forests and travel along the side of steep cliffs. The Palouse horses were spotted on their rumps and other places.

On my grandmother's side of the family, her father was Snake River-Nez Perce who made his living as a horse trader and accomplished gambler. He traded horses with Indians and settlers, but he also learned the white man's games of chance. And he was very successful gambling for high stakes his entire life. He made part of his living by gambling. I grew up hearing my grandmother tell stories about my relative who loved to deal in horses and gamble. My grandmother was not allowed to go down to her father's horse corrals when the Mexicans, Blacks, or Chinese came to trade horses with her father. I suspect that was because of her mother's and aunt's trepidation about what spirits those people might have with them to trade. Liquor was prohibited for Native people, and of course, Indian agents prohibited opium or any other hallucinogenic like mezcal. And those were valuable items in Indian Country, because they were contraband.

My grandmother used to talk about white horse traders visiting the family and bargaining with grandmother's dad. She talked of white horse traders who visited her father on business bringing bags of horehound candy that they tossed to children, including my grandmother and her sister. If my grandmother's father knew the people coming to visit and deal in horses, he would allow his girls to visit the corrals to observe the horse trading. My grandmother and her sister grew up on horseback and I like to remind myself that when Lewis and Clark came to our country, they said men and women here could ride equally well. And that is still true today on our reservation. There are men and women who compete athletically, whether it is in relay races, roping, barrel racing, bronc riding, or other competitive equine sports. Native American men and women throughout the Plateau participate in horse-related events.

The first people of the Columbia Plateau are part of a national horse culture that once enveloped the entire region. However, the invasion of our homelands by settlers and theft of lands through the treaties reduced our population to a remnant of a once great horse culture. I say remnant because the Indian people of the Plateau once controlled all the land and resources. Once the federal government confined us onto the reservations and settlers claimed nearly all the lands that once belonged to us, our horse populations declined. Added to this, during the wars of the 1850s, Chief Tilcoax of the Snake River-Palouse lost approximately one thousand horses when the United States Army slaughtered his horse herd, leaving the dead animals to decay on the present-day border of Washington and Idaho just east of Spokane, Washington. The Wolf family is part of our reservation, and they are directly related to Tilcoax and his son, Wolf Necklace. They were great horse people recognized throughout the Pacific Northwest for their quality Cayuse horses. Chief Tilcoax was not the only person to lose his horse herd. During the war and in its aftermath, settlers stole Indian horses and sheriffs confiscated horses for grazing on lands claimed by settlers, counties, and the states.

The Indigenous people of the Plateau continue their relationship with horses, including me. I selectively bred an Appaloosa stallion from Farmington, New Mexico, who came from breeding stock out of the King Ranch of Texas. Some racing horses were in that family tree. I selectively bred that Appaloosa stallion with a quarter horse mare that had top and bottom bred Peppy San badger bloodlines. I bred these two horses because I wanted the lankiness and the conformation of the horse to be produced to be more of the size of Cayuse horses our people selectively bred for in the past. So, I took a fifteen hand, one-inch mare and selectively bred her to a sixteen hand Appaloosa stud. The result was a horse, and ultimately horses, that are fifteen to sixteen hands high. The horses resulting from that breeding are ground-smart—not spooky or lightheaded. They are smart, sound on the ground, intelligent horses who are loyal to the people they carry. I'm very happy with the byproduct of the selective breeding I did about fifteen years ago. My horse herd today is of the highest quality and much like the original Cayuse horse of the eighteenth and nineteenth centuries.

Today, our reservations are postage stamp-sized compared to our once great homeland of millions of acres. Our land holdings were vast, and we enjoyed vast pastures, water resources, and freedom to move our herds across the Plateau. Today, our Umatilla Reservation is less than two thousand acres. This dramatic change in range lands ruined our horse culture our people once knew. Still, horses remain important to citizens of all the reservation populations in the Inland Northwest. Today, our concerns focus on reservations centers on raising our economic prosperity, improving our health, and general wellbeing of our people. In addition to needing land to raise horses, you must have enough money to race horses, participate in rodeos, pay for veterinary care, shoeing, feed, and supplements.

Our reservation citizens work for a living, and many couples must pay for childcare, food, and other common familial necessities. So, if you are raising horses on a reservation today, you must have sufficient disposable income to properly care for your horses. Our families with horses depend on their entire families to care for their horses. Those of us who own horses continue to use them for camping, herding, hunting, fishing, gathering, and riding for fun. Families with horses recreate on reservation lands and ride them deep into the mountains where we once lived. Horses also play important roles in our memorial processions honoring our ancestors.

Horses are still common sights on Indian reservations in the Northwest, but it is not as easy as it used to be to own horses. In the recent past, we had more land, and more time, and more resources dedicated to horses. Yet, horses have been significant to the Indigenous people of the Columbia Plateau for a long time, and they remain important to us today.

10

CARRIE JIM SCHUSTER

THE CREATOR'S GIFTS

Mary Jim and Carrie Jim Schuster (c. 1980)
Richard Scheuerman Photograph

Matriarch Carrie Jim Schuster of the Snake River-Palouse grew up along the lower Snake River in the vicinity of Ice Harbor before the construction of dams in the area in the 1950s and '60s. She was raised speaking Palouse Sahaptin and followed a traditional lifeway before flooding caused by the dams forced Jim family members to relocate to area reservations. She spent considerable time during her youth on the Umatilla Reservation in the household of prominent elder Annie Hair Johnson, one of the founders of the Pendleton Roundup. Carrie attended Riverside Indian School in Anadarko, Oklahoma, and graduated from Central Washington University in communications and from Heritage University with a graduate degree in education.

Carrie assisted Virginia Beavert in compiling oral histories for Anakú Iwachá: Yakama Legends and Stories (1974), and was a principal consultant for the Snake River-Palouse histories from Washington State University Press Renegade Tribe *(1986) and* River Song *(2015). A tireless advocate of Indigenous rights and environmental protection, she and her mother, Mary Jim Chapman, also provided expert congressional testimony to the Senate Select Committee on Indian Affairs regarding the Native American Graves Protection and Repatriation Act and Northwest Indian fisheries.*

The Creator's Gifts (2015)

Oral histories and myths like the ones in this collection that my mother, Mary Jim, and others like Andrew George and Gordon Fisher shared over the years have long been told to create awareness in young and old alike about our place in the world. The lives of all creatures are beautifully woven in the fabric of life, from the tiniest insects, butterflies, and moths to the larger creatures like beaver and salmon. The water and earth they inhabit is also here to sustain us.

Our tribal elders reminded us of the old prophecies and warnings about what will happen if we neglect our responsibilities as stewards of the land. Today we experience some of the consequences from this neglect. My mother and the Fishers, Georges, and others like them faced shared challenges because we grew up living freely in our ancestral lands. Only later in life were families like ours confined to the reservation, long after I had begun my education from my parents, aunts, uncles, and other elders.

***Tamayxplá* ("Wind Against the River") Village and**
***Uuša'ayt* ("Gambling Place") Racetrack Area**
Big Flat Wildlife Habitat Unit at Dalton Lake
Northeast of Pasco, Washington

I was raised in camps along the Snake River as our ancestors had lived for generations with the bounty of the river and land sufficient for all our needs. Only with the flooding of our home after the building of Ice Harbor Dam were we forced to move to the reservation. Through the courage and faith of elders like my mother we made a new life, but our hearts are still back home and we return there every year.

Having that natural world cut off was a great sorrow, and the elders sought each other's presence to deal with the loss of the life we knew. They remembered the cruel way in which so many older ones had left this life, but found strength in the words of our prophets at Priest Rapids—Yúyuni, Šmuhalla, and on back in time. After humanity's fall in the ancient time the people repented and our prophets told us how to follow the Creator's way by honoring the sacred foods—water, roots, salmon, berries, venison. He fashioned their images in the petroglyphs along the Snake River and at Priest Rapids as instruction for the people. Those stones are sacred so we did not touch them.

Our prophets taught us not to waste the Creator's gifts but to honor them in order to sustain the people. They fasted at sacred places like Rattlesnake Mountain for visions and strength, and we learned the stories of such places:

In the time before the Animal People,

Áan—Sun, had five wives
 as was customary back then.
His wives were Rattlesnake Mountain and three sisters—
 Mt. Adams, Mt. St. Helens, and Mt. Hood.
Rattlesnake Mountain was Sun's favorite wife.
As sunrise appeared each morning in the east,
 he first loved her.
At that time she was as tall and beautiful
 as the great Cascade peaks,
  and cast a shadow upon the other mountains.
The four sisters grew jealous of Sun's attention,
 and wanted him to spend more time with them.
They talked it over and decided to destroy his favorite.
One day after Sun had passed overhead
 they attacked Rattlesnake Mountain
  and pounded her down in a terrible fight.
When Sun arose the next day,
 and saw what had happened,
  he mourned the loss of his beloved
   and rain fell upon the earth for many days.
Sun gathered Rattlesnake Mountain's remaining hazel
 and pine nuts,

her camas roots and huckleberries,
> and spread them around his remaining wives.
But Sun still loved his disfigured wife,
> and left around her beautiful stands of balsamroot
> and lupine for the coming people,
>> and *piyax̣í, anipä́c, sawítk,*
>> and some roots that only grow there.

The lessons taught to us by elders like my mother, Andrew, and Gordon are not only about our people's covenant with the Almighty. They are also offered as a guide to others who care about our world because this natural law takes precedence over the commercial exploitation of resources given to us by the Creator. If we follow our elders' examples as stewards of the land then our children and grandchildren will benefit. But misuse threatens their future through contamination of our water, air, and land which affects everyone's food and health. There is so much pollution and noise today that young people today do not recognize the sound of the earth and what it is telling us.

**Wánawiš—Horn Rapids Fishery and Rattlesnake Mountain
John Clement Photograph**

Back on the Snake River where I was raised we lived with the fish and animals. There were lots of beavers living all over. They made pools in the streams to cleanse the water, trees grew along the riverbanks and cooled the water for the salmon, and we had safe places to play. The animals were put here to do these things and to teach us. But now our rivers and streams have become nothing but lifeless reservoirs and concrete canals. These are the kinds of things my mother, Andrew, and Gordon would mourn. They remembered the days of no dams on the river and no paved roads across our lands—the way God had made it.

Gordon was wise because he listened to his grandparents who told about their everyday experiences in the Palouse and on the Snake River before their life on the reservation. He also learned from them to be a man of peace. When he was young he lived for a time with Cleveland Kamiakin and his wife, Alalumt'i, in Nespelem and learned from them and others like Charlie Williams about the old ways. Gordon attended the Longhouse with the men and he would listen to them talk. Cleveland and Charlie and Camille Williams would tell about Chief Kamiakin and Chief Joseph. He also spent time with his Fisher grandparents, Sam and Helen, at the old village of *Palus* on the Snake River.

Andrew George was a Longhouse spiritual leader, and the first time I saw Andrew George was when he was visiting with Robert Burke from Umatilla at Wówniyu's place where we stayed after coming to the reservation. They loved smelt and fresh muffins so I worked to make them just right—rolled in corn meal and cooked on a wood stove. Andrew went on to also become a leader in the All-Tribes Church. He knew the spiritual truths that form the foundation for the well-being of children and grandchildren. No whip-man was needed when Andrew was around. He was a disciplinarian but never needed to execute his power! Everyone respected him.

We were trained to be silent in the elders' presence and to listen—no playing the radio or making noise. They taught us to be still—something

Left: *Katúmqal* Cedar Root Storage Basket
Right: *Wówniyu* Root–digger Horn Handle and Cedar Root Baskets
Carrie Jim Schuster Collection/John Clement Photographs

they learned from their parents during the war times, and they passed that on down to us. Our elders knew the beautiful life we all once shared, and at the center of that beauty was the family. We learned how our families were all related from the time we all lived together along the river. These are relationships that go back many generations.

My hope is that others will benefit from these teachings, and to avoid thinking that unlimited exploitation and technology bring only progress. May they benefit from the lessons of those who inhabited this land since time immemorial, and understand that rivers and trees and animals also have their place in the circle of life. Appreciation and respect for this knowledge represent real hope for our shared future.

11

SAM PAMBRUN

MISSIONS AND MÉTIS

Retired Ft. Nez Percés Father–Son Traders
Andrew and Alexander Pambrun
Pambrun Farm on the Umatilla Indian Reservation (c. 1885)
Sam Pambrun Collection

Historian-educator Sam Pambrun is a descendant of Canadien fur traders who came to the Oregon Country in 1823. His ancestor Pierre-Chrysologue Pambrun who was put in charge of Fort Nez Percés ("Old Fort Walla Walla") near the confluence of the Columbia and Walla Walla Rivers in 1832. Under his able administration the station became a critical link between Ft. Vancouver and the inland posts of

Ft. Colville and Ft. Hall. Pambrun fostered good relations with area tribal leaders and befriended many explorers, missionaries, and others prominent in Northwest frontier history. Pierre Pambrun's son, Andrew, served as clerk and trader at Ft. Walla Walla in the 1840s and '50s, and served as an interpreter at the 1855 Walla Walla Treaty Council.

Sam Pambrun served as an Oregon public school teacher and administrator and as curriculum director for the Umatilla-Morrow Educational Service District. He has also a past president of the Frenchtown Historic Foundation and Umatilla County Historical Society. He has written extensively on regional history themes and resides in Pendleton, Oregon.

St. Rose of Frenchtown (2015)

The first Oregon Territory Catholic Missions established east of the Cascade Mountains were founded as a result of persistent solicitation by French Canadian, Métis (mixed-blood) employees of early fur trade companies. These included workers for John Jacob Astor's Pacific Fur Company, Canadian North West Company, and British Hudson's Bay Company. Métis fur trade employees often "married" local native women and lived among their in-laws. This is true of the Frenchtown community (established 1823) in the Walla Walla Valley and French Prairie (1830) in the Willamette Valley. As the Canadian fur traders retired they built permanent homes and sought the comfort of their traditional lifestyles. Métis traditional lifestyle included Catholic spiritual guidance, validation of their marriages, baptism of their children, and access to the sacraments.

Prior to the arrival of missionaries, the mixed-blood employees of Fort Nez Percés, a trading post at Wallula, Washington, and residents of the Walla Walla Valley community of Frenchtown conducted Catholic catechism lessons for their Native American customers and their families. On the eve of the 1848 Cayuse War they finally succeeded in persuading the Church to send Catholic missionaries and teachers across the continent to serve the Métis of Walla Walla. This was their second try; the first Catholic missionaries to Oregon and Washington settled west of the Cascade Mountains.

The Frenchtown residents' benefactor, the Hudson's Bay Company, was an English commercial establishment chartered in 1670 in North America for the purpose of acquiring furs used in the manufacture of top hats. The HBC relied almost exclusively on French Canadien (French spelling) engagés to perform the work of trapping, trading and transporting beaver and other furs from the hinterlands to market. As such, the HBC attempted to accommodate the men whose lives of hardship could be eased somewhat by exporting Catholic missionaries to Oregon. This gesture of goodwill, however, resulted in a seismic collision between Protestants and Catholics on the western frontier.

Five missions named "St. Rose" were established in Eastern Washington amid the cultural turmoil and Indian Wars of the mid-nineteenth century. At the Frenchtown Historic Site two miles west of the Whitman Mission a twenty-foot marble obelisk and a twenty-foot

Frenchtown St. Rose Mission Obelisk

wooden cross commemorate the first Catholic missions on the Columbia Plateau. The cross establishes the place as a Christian cemetery. The obelisk contains the names of some of the earliest Oregon settlers.

The first Catholic missionaries to reach Frenchtown were Vicar General to the Bishop of Quebec Francois Xavier Norbert Blanchet and his associate Father Modeste Demers. Abbé Blanchet left Montreal on April 17, 1838, bound for what was then known as the "Oregon Country." Blanchet had been appointed to minister to the to the natives and Métis of Oregon by Joseph Provencher, Bishop of Juliopolis at St. Boniface, Red River Colony (now Winnipeg, Manitoba). The Reverend Provencher was an impressive man, 6' 4" in his stocking feet and black robe. He'd established St. Boniface the summer of 1818.

Blanchet traveled to Red River by Hudson's Bay Company "Brigade." A Brigade consisted of a flotilla of slow, heavy-laden canoes that each transported a ton of "outfit" or trade goods and supplies across the rivers, creeks, lakes and ponds of North America. On the return trip the Brigade transported 90-pound fur bales out to market. These slow boats were usually paddled by a crew of 6 to 8 mixed-blood Canadiens, people Abbé Blanchet was going west to serve. Blanchet joined the Brigade at Montreal, traveled up the Ottawa River and over a series of portages to Lake Superior, across it and another series of portages to Lake Winnipeg. From Lake Winnipeg the Brigade paddled fifty miles up the Red River to meet Bishop Provencher at St. Boniface Mission.

There Abbé Blanchet also met his future traveling companion and colleague, Father Modeste Demers. Demers had been ordained the year before. The two priests were detained for five weeks, enjoying an unexpected adventure as they accompanied the Red River Métis on their summer buffalo hunt. They traversed the prairies in Red River carts in search of buffalo, the staple of the plains. The buffalo were killed, butchered and the meat dried (smoked), pounded to shreds, salted and mixed with berries to make an almost indestructible food known as "pemmican." The pemmican was placed in buffalo hide bags between layers of melted buffalo fat. The 90-pound bags would keep for five years or more. Pemmican was the high-protein food that fueled the fur trade boat rowers as they crisscrossed North America.

**Earthen Remnant of the Hudson's Bay Brigade Route and
Oregon Trail Extension to Ft. Nez Percés
Sam Pambrun Photograph**

Abbé Blanchet and Father Demers left Red River July 10, 1838, on the "Express." As opposed to the Brigade, the Express was composed of fast, light canoes that carried the mail, light cargo, and important Hudson's Bay officers and guests. They paddled down Red River, across Lake Winnipeg to Norway House, up the Saskatchewan River to Fort Carlton, Fort Edmonton and up the Athabasca River to Jasper House. At Jasper they traded their boats for horses to cross the crest of the Rocky Mountains, arriving at "Boat Encampment" on the Columbia River October 13. From Boat Encampment Blanchet and Demers took to boats again, this time flat-bottomed plank boats called "bateau."

On October 21 at a place then called *Dalles des Morts*, just above HBC's Fort Colvile, one of the Express boats overturned in the rapids causing a dozen fatalities. Chief Trader Archibald McDonald sent help from Fort Colvile. Abbé Blanchet and Father Demers conducted the last rights and interments and consoled the survivors. Continuing down the Columbia the Express made short stops at Forts Okanagan and Nez Percés (later called Fort Walla Walla) and arrived at Fort Vancouver in late November.

At Fort Nez Percés Blanchet baptized the children of Jacques Servant. He had been employed at the Fort since 1831. During the next eight years Blanchet and Demers established missions in the Willamette and Cowlitz Valleys, on the lower Columbia River and at Nesqualy (original spelling). They recruited additional priests (DeSmet, et. al.), nuns from the order Sisters of Notre Dame de Namur, and hired lay persons to manage their missions and native schools. To accomplish this, Blanchet and Demers were continually fund raising, even at the Vatican in Rome. They traveled the Pacific Northwest extensively, making promises to open additional missions. Numerous times they heard, loud and clear, the wishes of Frenchtown residents that the Holy Father send priests to the Walla Walla Valley.

Restored "The Prince's Cabin" (c. 1837) at Frenchtown

At the time the Walla Walla Valley was the domain of the Cayuse and Marcus and Narcissa Whitman who had located their Presbyterian

Mission at *Waiilatpu* the fall of 1836. *Waiilatpu* is a Nez Perce and Cayuse word for "Place of Rye Grass." *Waiilatpu* was surrounded by the Whitmans' neighbors, Métis who'd settled there a dozen years before Marcus and Narcissa arrived in 1836. The Whitmans did not have much empathy for the Canadiens of Frenchtown, occasionally referring to the children of their mixed-blood neighbors as "abominations." The Frenchtown Métis continued to agitate for Catholic teachers until Bishop Agustin Magloire Alexandre Blanchet (Francois Norbert's brother) and eight associate priests arrived in September 1847. Bishop Blanchet traveled 2000 miles from Quebec to St. Louis, arriving there the spring of 1847. This time the Hudson's Bay Company did not fund or sponsor the Catholic migration. Bishop Blanchet traveled the final 1,670 miles from St. Louis (Westport) to Walla Walla via the Oregon Trail on a 12-wagon train under the charge of Captain Wiggins.

Blanchet's first encounter with Marcus Whitman was an unpleasant affair at Fort Walla Walla. Blanchet was staying there, consulting with Chief Trader William McBean and roaming the countryside looking for places to build churches. Whitman was on his way home from negotiations with the Reverend H. K. W. Perkins to purchase his Methodist Mission at The Dalles. Even though The Dalles Mission was Methodist, Marcus was intimately familiar with it. Narcissa had fled there from *Waiilatpu* in October 1842 for protection after she was attacked by an unknown intruder while she was sleeping. She stayed with the Perkins and Daniel Lee families until Marcus returned from the east where he had been pleading with the American Board of Foreign Missions in Boston to reverse their closure order for his Walla Walla Valley Mission.

The Whitman–Blanchet meeting according to Bishop A. M. A. Blanchet:

> *It was on September 23rd [1847] at Fort Walla Walla, that I first saw Dr. Whitman. He was returning from The Dalles. He showed much displeasure at my arrival to these reaches. He spoke of religion, repeated the normal accusations against Catholics, reproached them*

for the alleged persecutions that the Protestants had endured at their hands & claimed that one need not be baptized to be a Christian; finally, that he knew why I had come: that Tawotoé had requested me, or rather it was due to his influence that I had been elected Bishop of Walla Walla!! That he was going to oppose me with all his power; that he didn't like Catholics; and for this reason, would come to our aid with food only if we were starving.

Towatoé (Tauitau) was called Young Chief by the Hudson's Bay Company. At the time, the HBC considered Tauitau the most influential Cayuse leader.

Whitman shouldered considerable responsibilities. His wife was not happy at *Waiilatpu* where she felt endangered. The Cayuse Indians were threatening and suffering from a measles epidemic. Whitman's missionary colleagues continued writing derogatory letters about him to the American Board of Missions, reporting he was incompetent and failing his responsibility to "convert" the Cayuse Indians. In addition, the Oregon Trail emigrants who were streaming through his mission were accusing him of price gouging. Meeting Bishop A. M. A. Blanchet at Fort Walla Walla did not improve matters for Whitman.

During October and November 1847 there were important, wide-ranging discussions at Fort Walla Walla, Frenchtown, Tauitau's village on the Umatilla, and Whitman's nearest neighbors at the Cayuse *Pásxa* village. *Pásxa* was located 300 yards east of the Whitman Mission compound boundary. The band leader at *Pásxa* was Umtiippe, the man who found little Clarissa Whitman in the Walla Walla River where she drowned. He cried when he couldn't revive her.

The discussion concerned where the Catholics should build a mission. Tiloukaikt, a serious opponent of the Whitmans who resided at *Pásxa*, first tried to give Bishop Blanchet and his associate Father Jean Baptiste Abraham Brouillet land adjacent to the Whitman Mission. Then Tiloukaikt changed his mind, saying what he was planning to give was too small, he would just chase off Whitman and give his mission to the Catholics. Bishop Blanchet and Father Brouillet refused Tiloukaikt's offer.

At Tauitau's invitation, Brouillet instead refurbished Tauitau's log house on the Umatilla River, twenty-five miles across the bunchgrass prairies from *Waiilatpu*. This house was built by Pierre Chrysologue Pambrun, Chief Trader at Fort Walla Walla, for Tauitau in 1837 as a peace settlement. Brouillet named his new mission St. Anne and moved in November 27, 1847, two days before the Cayuse killed Marcus and Narcissa Whitman and eleven others at *Waiilatpu*. When Father Brouillet learned of the murders, he traveled to *Waiilatpu* and buried the Whitmans and several others. He then returned to his new mission on the Umatilla. He promised to stay at St. Anne's if the Cayuse refrained from further violence against the whites. When they executed more *Waiilatpu* hostages Brouillet moved out. In retaliation, the Cayuse burned his mission.

The details and relationships of these events are difficult to follow. There were many actors from diverse cultures. Distance and time were important factors; St. Anne's and the Whitman Mission were a day's ride apart. Conventional wisdom in 1847 was much different from today's perspectives. Both Missions were situated in close proximity to large, permanent Cayuse villages. The twenty or so Cayuse bands and villages on the Umatilla and Walla Walla Rivers were all interrelated. Among these bands there was no "Head Chief" who could speak on behalf of all the Cayuse nor control their behavior.

Today the Catholic mission on the Umatilla Reservation is called St. Andrew's, the successor to St. Anne's. The site of Tauitau's house and the original St. Anne Mission is about a mile north of the Umatilla River, at the top of Thorn Hollow Grade on what is now known as the Shoeships Place. This location was verified by Sister Florita to historian Clifford Drury in 1970. It was located on the main Indian Road and sometimes Oregon Trail route between the Grande Ronde and Walla Walla Valleys. St. Anne's overlooked miles of bunchgrass and a thousand of Tauitau's horses.

The first St. Rose Mission was established in the Yakima Valley in 1847. Legend and most historians have located the first St. Rose Mission near the mouth of the Yakima River near present day Richland, Washington. The first St. Rose was built by Oblate of Mary Immaculate (OMI) Father Eugene Casimir Chirouse with permission of Walla Walla Chief PeoPeo MoxMox. This mission and several other 1847 Oblate Missions up and down the Yakima Valley were identified by Denys Nelson in his 1926 unpublished manuscript at the City of Vancouver, British Columbia Public Archives. Nelson described the missions of St. Rose of Chemna, St. Mary, Holy Cross (*Ste. Croix de Simkoué*) and St. Joseph.

The anonymous Catholic writer Historicus wrote that the first four baptisms were performed by Father Chirouse at the *Ste. Rose Mission at Camná* on November 30, 1847 (day after Whitman Massacre) and written in the baptismal record by Father Pandosy. In an unpublished manuscript, Bruce Rigsby and Greg Cleveland summarize all the research on the location of Yakima Valley Catholic Missions. They too conclude the first St. Rose was located at or near the mouth of the Yakima River, between the mouth and "The Horn." [An undated newspaper account from the *Tri-City Herald* (c. 1950) identified the location as the present Richland Riding Club Stables.]

A. J. Splawn in his 1917 book *Kamiakin, the Last Hero of the Yakimas* contends that *Chem-na* was a Yakima (Yakama) place name for "Mouth of the Yakima River" but he reported that St. Rose was first established at *Simkoe* further up the Valley near the "Old Shaker Church" at White Swan. This is the same place Nelson said St. Rose of Chemna was located. The distance between the mouth of the Yakima and Simcoe is about 100 miles, much too great a discrepancy to be attributed to a minor error in describing the site of something as unusual as a European church among the Yakama Nation.

Bishop Blanchet's journal complicates the issue:

Father Ricard selected a place called Simkoe *and left Father Chirouse in charge of the mission which they called St. Rose. During the following year, Father Chirouse followed the Indians as they moved from camp to camp and baptized sixteen children, thirteen adults and married nine couples, but had to leave during the winter of 1848 on account of the Cayuse War.*

Splawn reported that in October of 1847 Yakama Chief Kamiakin traveled to Walla Walla and escorted two priests back to his village in the upper Yakima Valley at *Ahtanum* where they established the St. Joseph Mission. In Splawn's words, "two Oblate fathers, E. C. Chirouse and Paschal Richard founded a mission at Kamiakin's village on the upper *Ah-tan-um*." Although none of the Yakima Valley missions lasted through the Cayuse War, each priest filed a 640-acre land claim for each mission. This was a formula the missionaries continued in the Walla Walla Valley.

Following the Whitman Massacre the Cayuse War ensued, bringing avengers from the Willamette Valley to Walla Walla. The *Pásxa* and other Cayuse villages cleared out as the militia chased Cayuse Indians all over the landscape for two years. Thirteen Cayuse men were eventually surrendered as being responsible for killing the Whitmans and five were hanged at Oregon City in 1850. All had relatives married to Canadiens at Frenchtown. The Catholic Métis of Frenchtown were blamed for inciting the massacre and for harboring the fugitives.

Peter Skene Ogden, HBC Chief Factor and bourgeois (merchant-traders) of Fort Vancouver came up the Columbia with boatloads of HBC gifts and trade goods to ransom fifty-six hostages who were being held at Cayuse villages in the vicinity of the Mission. Ogden was successful though he barely secured the hostages before the area was flooded with an unruly Oregon Volunteer Militia bent on revenge. It is likely that if the militia had reached the Walla Walla Valley before Ogden there would have been no hostages alive to ransom.

In 1853 Father Chirouse established a second St. Rose Mission, this one called St. Rose of the Cayouse and located at the confluence of Yellow Hawk Creek and the Walla Walla River. Recently, with permission of landowners Bob and Cindy Gregoire, the Frenchtown Historic Foundation commemorated the St. Rose of the Cayouse Mission site with an interpretive sign. Father Chirouse filed a 640-acre claim under the auspices of the 1850 Donation Land Act. His claim was later denied.

Father Chirouse's mission was constructed with Frenchtown labor. Harriet Duncan Munnick's *Catholic Church Records of the Pacific Northwest* volume on St. Anne, Walla Walla, and Frenchtown contains a pencil sketch of the St. Rose of the Cayouse Mission. The building was a type of construction known as a "dog-trot." One portion of the structure was living quarters, the other, connected by a common roof was usually the kitchen; in this case, the mission chapel.

St. Anne's Mission Drawing Based on Fr. Blanchet's Sketch (1847)
H. D. Munnick, *Catholic Church Records of the Pacific Northwest* (1972)

In December 1855 a second Indian War claimed the Yellow Hawk mission. The Battle of Walla Walla, fought at Frenchtown a few miles from the St. Rose of the Cayouse Mission resulted in the mission building being burned to the ground. The early writers of Oregon history blamed the Indians; later historians have speculated the Oregon Mounted Volunteers from the Willamette Valley were responsible for torching it.

This has been an unanswered question for 150 years. The volunteers were not immune to church-burning; a month earlier in November they had burned Father Pandosy's St. Joseph Mission on the *Ahtanum*.

A third St. Rose was established in 1863 on the William McBean Donation Land Claim two miles southwest of the original Yellow Hawk mission. This log chapel on the south bank of the Walla Walla River was used only a few months and was then relocated seven miles away to the north side of the Walla Walla River.

The fourth St. Rose Mission on the north bank was built in 1863 on the Narcisse Raymond land claim. This "new" 1863 church was located on what is now known as the Baker Ranch. Descendants of Charles Franklin Baker sold the ranch to Kelly and Susan Allen in 2012. It adjoins Frenchtown Historic Site. The fourth St. Rose was used intermittently for church services, a school and a community hall. Sometime before 1876 a Catholic school was built near the church. The Frenchtown Métis contributed a significant amount of time and money to construct facilities for itinerant priests and a school for their children. Cherri Baker Melnick and Craig Baker assisted in locating the 1863 cemetery and the sites of the St. Rose church and adjacent school.

There were seventeen recorded burials at the St. Rose of the Cayouse Cemetery, all Indians who had converted to Catholicism. The exact location of the St. Rose of the Cayouse Cemetery on Yellow Hawk Creek is unknown. The second Walla Walla Valley Catholic Cemetery was established at the Raymond place in 1863 and recorded eighteen burials through 1875, including Canadiens (Métis), baptized Indians and a few Americans. This cemetery washed away the winter of 1875-1876 and those who were recovered were re-interred on a knoll to the north in January of 1876. This cemetery on the knoll is known as the Frenchtown Cemetery.

The fifth and final St. Rose Mission was built in September 1876 on land donated by Marcel Gagnon. The Gagnon family had purchased a portion of the Narcisse Raymond land claim and, in turn, donated a part of it to the Catholic mission. The 1876 St. Rose of Lima Mission was built approximately 200 yards due west of the 1863 St. Rose Mission. St. Rose of Lima is now a part of the Frenchtown Historic Site and its "footprint" was verified by a team of archaeologists from Eastern Washington University in 2009. Frenchtown Historical Foundation commissioned the study. The St. Rose of Lima site is now situated on land donated to the Confederated Tribes of the Umatilla Reservation by the Frenchtown Historic Foundation.

Just west across the Frenchtown-Bergevin property line from St. Rose of Lima is another known footprint, the site of the Larocque Cabin. The Oregon Mounted Volunteers commandeered Joseph Larocque's house to use as their headquarters and hospital during the four-day 1855 Battle of Walla Walla. They executed Peopeo Moxmox there while holding him as a hostage. Twenty years later the St. Rose of Lima chapel could easily have been built on or very near the place where Peopeo Moxmox's body was hastily interred in the dark, the night of December 7, 1855. The St. Rose of Lima church building was dismantled in 1911 and the lumber used to build a grocery store at the corner of 9th and Chestnut Streets in Walla Walla.

Oregon Territory's first Catholic Diocese was at Oregon City. The second Diocese was at Nesqualy (present Nisqually). The Walla Walla Diocese was "erected" July 24, 1846, two months before Bishop Blanchet arrived in Oregon and was officially "suppressed" May 31, 1850, in favor of the Nesqualy Diocese. This was the only such suppression in the United States. By the early 1900s the community of Frenchtown was substantially "Americanized." Most of the original French Canadien Catholic inhabitants had fled to the Umatilla Indian Reservation where their spouses were allotted land under the Slater and Dawes Acts. Today, the city of Walla Walla, like its Frenchtown predecessor, is a vibrant, multi-cultural community, thanks in part, to traditions established by early Métis settlers who imported their religion and culture from Montreal to the Walla Walla Valley.

The Hudson's Bay Company Farm, 1821–1855 (2016)

Not many Walla Walla Valley enterprises have been in business for nearly 200 years. Historic Hudson's Bay Company Farm (now Williams Brothers Hudson Bay Farm) is such a place. Located a few miles west of Umapine, Oregon, the historic farm was established by the North West Company (NWC) of Montreal as early as 1818. When the NWC and the Hudson's Bay Company (HBC) merged in 1821, the farm became known as the Hudson's Bay Company Farm.

The HBC was chartered in 1670 by the King of England who granted a monopoly that allowed HBC officers to serve as governmental, judicial and military administrators for the geography contained in the charter. When the charter was amended to include that territory west of the Rocky Mountains known as "The Oregon Country," the HBC officers became the de facto government of the Pacific Northwest. There was not much to govern at first, just a few fur trading posts, a hundred or so mixed-blood employees, and the HBC Farm.

The first fur trading post on the Pacific Coast was built the summer of 1811 by John Jacob Astor's Pacific Fur Company. Fort Astoria soon expanded its operations up the Columbia, establishing posts at Okanagan, Spokane, and several others farther north. The NWC purchased the Pacific Fur Company in 1813. The NWC had been moving its operations west, crossing the Rocky Mountains in 1808. By the time they purchased Astoria they were already building fur trade posts on the Columbia watershed.

The NWC built Fort Nez Percés near the confluence of the Walla Walla and Columbia Rivers just west of present Wallula in 1818. About the same time, twenty miles up the Walla Walla Valley, the company established what became known as the HBC Farm. The original purpose of this property was to provide horses for the "Snake Brigades." These were traveling trapping companies composed of a hundred or so men, women, and children with 200 to 300 horses. Under the HBC, the Brigades' job was to trap out the upper Snake River and its tributaries and discourage American competition.

The HBC Farm was located in an ideal place to trade horses with area Indians who owned and pastured thousands in and around the Walla Walla Valley. Besides good grazing it also had rich soil and a temperate climate. The HBC Farm was located in proximity to the Cayuse Village of *Pásxa* and later community of Frenchtown and other Walla Walla villages further down the valley, but still at a respectful distance. It seems like the farm was purposefully sited so it would not encroach on Indian or Métis settlements.

There is a tendency in contemporary times to romanticize the early fur traders, describing them as happy-go-lucky French Canadiens, stern Scotsmen, trappers who wore buckskins and waded in icy streams, or rough men who "married" local Indian women. But make no mistake, first and foremost, fur trading companies and their employees represented large, wealthy, profit-oriented businesses. They had payrolls to meet, capital to raise, stockholders and customers to please, transportation systems and supply lines to work out, and a web of laws, rules, and regulations to follow. The HBC Farm was such a commercial enterprise and grew to be a vital part of the HBC's intricate support system for their far-flung Oregon Country Empire during the period 1821-1855.

FORT NEZ PERCÉS

The site of Fort Nez Percés was first visited by Europeans when Lewis and Clark passed along the Columbia River in 1805 and 1806. David Thompson of the North West Company planted a flag near the confluence of the Snake and Columbia Rivers in July of 1811 and claimed the Columbia and all the land it drained for the British. He promised the Indians he would build a trading post there. The Pacific Fur Company established the Walla Walla Rendezvous at the confluence of the Walla Walla and Columbia Rivers in 1812.

John Mix Stanley, *Old Fort Walla Walla* (Ft. Nez Percés), 1853
Issac Stevens, *Narrative and Final Report of Explorations*, Vol. 12 (1860)

The NWC built, or at least enclosed, Fort Nez Percés in 1818 but got off to a shaky start. Local Walla Walla and Snake River-Palouse Indians threatened violence; they were not happy about a foreign invasion without their consent. Not only was a structure being built on their land without payment, they were also being denied access to a place they had previously visited with impunity. With the fur traders planning to lock the gate, the Indians would have to request permission to enter the stockade. This was insulting to the Indians; construction was halted for weeks while an agreement was negotiated.

Donald McKenzie of the NWC had attempted to build Fort Nez Percés at the mouth of the Walla Walla River in 1814 but was stymied by Duncan McDougall, his frugal boss at Fort George (Astoria). He eventually went over his superior's head to build the post. According to Pambrun Family oral history, a small house, corrals, and a storage building were constructed on the end of the Snake River delta near the mouth of the Walla Walla in 1816. These structures periodically flooded. McKenzie, Alexander Ross, and ninety-five Métis and Kanaka (Hawaiian) laborers built the fort in two and a half months. Ross said he selected the site for the post and in 1820 began pasturing horses for McKenzie's Snake Brigade "up-stream" (Walla Walla).

The Brigades were large pack trains or flotillas, or sometimes both, that were designed to carry tons of "outfit" and "returns" to and from interior posts to ports on both the Atlantic and Pacific Coasts. Outfits were the trade goods and supplies needed to acquire furs from the Indians and to construct and maintain fur trade posts. Returns were the product, the furs the HBC shipped to London and sold to fur merchants. The Express mail and cargo boats followed the same routes as the Brigades, only much faster. The Express also carried officers and sometimes their families to and from posts scattered all over North America.

The HBC headquarters at Fort Vancouver continually pressured the Fort Nez Percés bourgeois for more and more horses, and for farming and transporting to and from Fort Nisqually on Puget Sound. The Columbia-Okanagan-Fraser supply line to New Caledonia (Northern British Columbia) and the Snake Brigade to the headwaters of the Snake River each required a hundred or more horses a year. The Hudson's Bay Farm was responsible for acquiring these horses, for taming and training them to pack, as well as for constructing pack saddles and tack.

The HBC also found another important function for Fort Nez Percés: "Security of the Communication." The post was midway on the Columbia River between Vancouver and Okanagan, a distance of about 600 miles. Communication up and down the Columbia, from post to headquarters and post to post was fundamental to the conduct of business. The HBC had lots of moving parts; safe and reliable communication was vital which made the Fort Nez Percés clerk's job especially important. When the Express arrived he stayed up all night frantically reading letters, reports, logs and journals, and copied those that contained information pertinent to the post. The boat usually left at dawn the next morning.

Fort Nez Percés lacked adjacent land for growing food or raising and housing stock. It was on the Brigade water route, built on the delta of the Walla Walla River on a peninsula projecting out into the Columbia. It featured sand, sagebrush, and prickly pear cactus. All vegetation around the fort was removed for security purposes. The HBC Farm was essential to the operations of this isolated post in such a barren environment. Fort Nez Percés could not function, or even exist, without its support system.

GOVERNOR (SIR) GEORGE SIMPSON

During 1824 and 1825 Hudson's Bay Company Governor (Sir) George Simpson made a whirlwind tour of the Pacific Northwest. He left the Hudson's Bay Company headquarters at York Factory on Canada's Hudson's Bay and traveled over 2500 miles west to Astoria, visiting company posts all along the way. Simpson typically managed by "walking around," and his favorite management tool was cutting costs. The reason for his tour of the Oregon Country was a recent British royal crown decree extending the HBC charter to the west side of the Rocky Mountains and selecting a new site for the Columbia Department's headquarters.

Along his route Simpson found many "inefficiencies," including "high living" at Spokane House. The employees there were enjoying imported "eatables, drinkables and other Domestic Comforts." Simpson remedied this by reorganizing the company district and issuing an edict that, "no longer will food be imported from London to sustain Company employees and their families." He closed Spokane House and replaced it with Fort Colvile (better farmland and on the main stem Columbia), replaced Fort George (Astoria) with Fort Vancouver as Columbia Department headquarters because of better farmland, but left Fort Nez Percés alone. Simpson likely recognized the potential of the HBC Farm for growing food crops, orchards, and raising livestock.

Simpson visited the HBC Farm, left some precious seed wheat and reminded the employees there that their dinner tables would no longer include imported food. He also significantly cut the company's regional workforce. After Simpson's visit, the Iroquois, Mohawks and other Indian employees who had been hired east of Rockies simply walked home. The Hawaiians were shipped out and the Métis, many of whom were in debt to the company, just sheltered in place and eventual became known as "freemen."

Freemen did not have employment contracts but were often attached to the company through debt and habit. The HBC extended credit to those who manned their Snake Brigades, and likely to their counterparts, sharecroppers on the HBC Farm. Although freemen were not carried on the company's rolls and received neither company benefits nor retirement, they performed work at the company's direction. Simpson was satisfied with this arrangement although Columbia Department post managers all complained of the difficulties they had in supervising the freemen. However, the "debt servitude" notion, long thought of as business as usual for the HBC, may not be entirely true. Research by historian Tom Holloway has revealed that most employees were in debt, but very few owed enough not to just "walk away." Fur trade conventional wisdom may need further examination.

Governor Simpson's cost-cutting measures placed considerable pressure on what was left of the staff at the HBC Farm to grow enough food to support Fort Nez Percés and other Columbia posts. Simpson also reduced the company quota of eight paddlers on Columbia River upstream *batteau* (flat-bottomed boats) to seven, and set a per boat cargo quota of fifty "pieces" at ninety pounds each, for a total of 4500 pounds per boat. This plagued Métis middlemen (paddlers) for years.

The HBC was a hierarchal organization. Employees were contracted for a specific time period and were sometimes called "servants." This military style, rank-conscious arrangement periodically fostered contentious responses. Colorful Ft. Spokane chief trader Finan McDonald, for example, wrote to Governor Simpson: "Your Laws and regalasion on the other side of the mountain give People a fright on this side." McDonald Road in today's Walla Walla Valley is named for Finan's ancestors.

FUR TRADE AGRICULTURE

To accommodate Governor Simpson's "grow your own" edict, the HBC Farm began raising food crops as well as cutting native grass hay. It was also prudent to fence out Indian horses and stock from the cultivated fields. Additional "gardens" were established. The descriptions, locations, and sizes of these gardens vary, but evidence suggests there were two substantial "gardens" in addition to the Hudson's Bay Farm. The first of these places was two miles up the Walla Walla River from Fort Nez Percés, just above today's Marie Dorion Park near Wallula. The second garden was located about four miles upstream where the "road" crossed the river to the mouth of Vancycle Canyon. Reported sizes of the gardens vary from four to fifty acres and both were fenced. Narcissa Whitman described the HBC gardens as "verdant" in 1836.

Ft. Nez Percés "Two-Mile Garden"
Present-day Walla Walla River Location

She listed some of the crops: melons, potatoes, and corn. Both gardens and the Hudson's Bay Farm likely had orchards.

Beside North Shore Road, just north of modern Wallula, one can still see the ruts of the HBC Road from Fort Nez Percés to the upper Walla Walla Valley. The Two-Mile Garden site is still visible, a mud flat created by the backwaters of McNary Dam. The HBC Road up the Walla Walla eventually became the Oregon Trail, connecting the Whitman Mission with Fort Nez Percés. Historian T. C. Elliot wrote that Washington Governor I. I. Stevens "went over the trail connecting the Wallula post with the branch institution (HBC Farm) in the year 1853. He spent the night there."

Describing frontier agriculture is problematic. Most of period reports and "mentions" of the HBC Farm do not delineate between the gardens and farm. The varieties and sizes of crops, herds, dwelling houses, barns, sheds, and corrals referred to in original documents may be aggregate numbers or may be referring to just the Hudson's Bay Farm. In addition, the reports vary based on who was reporting, to whom, for what purpose, and when. Figuring out which statistics apply to the Hudson's Bay gardens and which to the farm is presently an imprecise endeavor.

In his book *Farming the Frontier*, historian James R. Gibson provides substantial quantified data on the Hudson's Bay Farm in the Walla Walla Valley. In the late 1820s, for example, 250 horses were annually purchased at Fort Nez Percés in addition to the 50-100 already residing at the farm. Gibson also reports that Two-Mile Garden cultivated fifty acres in 1841 but only twelve acres in 1845. According to Gibson, the farm up the valley cultivated 30 acres in 1846. His table of livestock at Hudson's Bay Farm for 1826 shows twenty-four horses, but no cows, pigs, or poultry. The same table for 1846 shows 115 horses, thirty-six cattle, thirty-eight pigs, and some poultry. In another Gibson book, *Lifeline of the Oregon Country*, is found this passage from a John McLoughlin letter: "In the summer of 1836 some seventy horses were required from Walla Walla and bourgeois Pambrun was instructed to purchase as many horses as you can at a moderate price."

Other agriculture data includes Archibald McKinney's report that he traded 200-500 horses annually and normally kept 50-100 cows. McKinney was the factor in charge of Fort Nez Percés from 1841 to 1846. American physician and naturalist John Kirk Townsend visited the Columbia in 1834 and reported, "Pambrun raises potatoes, turnips, carrots and his Indian corn produces 80 bushels to the acre." Townsend was likely describing Four-Mile Garden. British Lieutenants Henry Warre and Mervin Vavasour created a table titled "Number of employees, cultivated acreage, and number of livestock at the posts of the Hudson's bay Company in the Columbia Department 1845." Their table lists Fort Nez Percés as having ten employees, twelve cultivated acres, twenty-three cattle, sixty-eight horses, and a dozen pigs. An HBC inventory shows that in the spring of 1844 "4 new ploughs" (plows) and "2 plough harnesses" were shipped to Fort Nez Percés.

Since we have only found one reference to hay at the HBC Farm it can be assumed grass hay was cut for the animals on the farm. Horses purchased for the Brigades were likely branded and allowed to run loose until needed, wintering on the dried bunch grass of the surrounding hills.

"FIFTY-FOUR FORTY OR FIGHT"

In 1818 the British-American "Convention of Commerce between His Majesty and the United States of America" was signed. This treaty, among other things, established the boundary between Canada and the United States at the 49th Parallel from the Atlantic Ocean to the "Stoney Mountains." West of the Rockies, the treaty provided for "Joint Occupation," the name by which the treaty is often referred. Joint Occupation meant the British and Americans were awarded equal access to the Oregon County. The treaty was renewed in August 1826 and expired on the last day of December 1845. When the Hudson's Bay

Company merged with the North West Company, the British, through the HBC Charter, were able to exercise almost complete control over the Pacific Northwest for next thirty-five years. As the treaty neared its end, competition for ownership of the Oregon Country nearly resulted in war.

This competition for the joint occupation lands had been building for twenty years. First American trappers were accused of "encroaching" on what the British thought of as their trapping grounds. Later, American missionaries began agitating for an "American" government in Oregon. And finally, when thousands of American pioneers began pouring into the Willamette Valley, it became impossible for the British to "hold" the territory. In 1831 Scottish botanist David Douglas was paid to advise the British Colonial Office on the best land for agriculture, commerce and where best, to serve British interests, to establish the boundary line. By the 1840s, the Americans, in response to over twenty years of boundary settlement rhetoric, had coined a rallying call, "54-40 or Fight!"

The United States Government sent Naval Lieutenant Charles Wilkes to Oregon in 1841 and John C. Fremont in 1843. The British sent Army officers Warre and Vavasour in 1845 to reconnoiter a military route and the logistics needed for moving troops into the Pacific Northwest. Both countries were anticipating military action. The British and American "scouts" covered the Northwest, even estimating the number of buffalo it would take to feed their marching armies. Both scouting parties checked out the HBC Farm in the Walla Walla Valley and collected data on crops, land under cultivation, livestock, and personnel. Both estimated what and how long it would take to grow enough food there to feed their respective armies. The June 15, 1846, US-Canada Boundary Settlement made these military preparations unnecessary.

THE GRANITE BOULDER

In 1965 two brass plaques, fastened to a granite boulder (probably a Missoula Flood erratic) were erected at the intersection of Umapine and Hudson Bay Roads approximately four miles west of the small Oregon town of Umapine. The upper plaque reads:

This plaque commemorates the Hudson's Bay Company Farm 1821-1856 where 500 head of horses and 100 cattle were run. The farm was bounded by the Snake River on the north, Blue Mountains on the east, Umatilla River on the south and the Columbia River on the west. Erected by the Hudson Bay Grange 1965, Grange established 1906.

Hudson's Bay Farm Present-day Location near Umapine, Oregon

The area encompassing that described on the plaque is millions of acres so seems somewhat exaggerated. However, the Grange had a legitimate, if not accurate source. Archibald McKinley, post manager at Fort Nez Percés, deposed these exact boundaries for the Hudson's Bay Company Farm in his testimony before an 1862 court. These proceedings were from the Hudson's Bay Company's lawsuit against the United States for recovery of depredations committed during the 1855 Battle of Frenchtown. The bottom brass plaque is missing but its text is known. It describes the date, the members of the Hudson Bay Grange Monument Committee, "verifies" that their information on the Hudson's Bay Farm came from the *Walla Walla Union Bulletin* newspaper, and describes where the boulder was originally found. Umatilla County Commissioner Ray Bevans was chair of the monument committee.

A June 19, 1938 *Walla Walla Union Bulletin* article by "roving reporter" A. W. Nelson describes a safari of Ed Hoon, Ed Hodgen, and K. A. Mays of Milton, Oregon, and Henry Barrett of Athena to find the exact location of the old Hudson's Bay Farm. According to the *Union Bulletin*, "Hoon and Hodgen led the group unhesitatingly to a spot in a hayfield about 200 yards from the farm home known variously as the Billie Goodman and Grant Lowe place." This "spot" is now occupied by a monument to the historic HBC Farm, on a granite boulder. It is in a triangle formed by the intersection of Umapine and Hudson Bay Roads, 200 yards northwest of the "old" farmhouse. The house is still standing, the oldest building on the place, and supposedly contains a log structure Billie Goodman built his framed house around. The house and boulder are surrounded by hayfields.

ON THE GROUND

The previous owners of the historic HBC Farm site, according to the *Union Bulletin*, include a man named Gohlson who originally homesteaded it, and Jim Fruit who bought it from Gohlson and then sold it to W. S. (Billie) Goodman. The latter's heirs sold it to Grant Lowe. The Williams family bought it from Lowe and has owned and farmed it for three generations. Early accounts describe the place as a "paradise of green" in the late summer and fall. The Oregon Trail emigrants who passed it on their way to the Whitman Mission must have enjoyed a respite here; several mentioned it in their diaries.

There is considerable difference between the area's spring-fed and snow-fed waterways. Most contemporary accounts of the Hudson's Bay Farm describe it as being on Pine Creek. This is misleading; the historic Hudson's Bay Company Farm was located near Pine Creek, but irrigated from Schwartz Creek. Goodman called Schwartz Creek "Spring Creek." It is unknown how Schwartz Creek got its name. The modern search for the "exact location" of the HBC farm and buildings began with this premise: drinking water and water for irrigation is best taken from year-around spring-fed waterways, not snow-fed creeks and rivers which are swollen torrents in March and April and dry in the late summer. Schwartz Creek is such a spring-fed creek. Pine Creek, on the other hand, is a muddy torrent in the spring of the year. Its headwaters are in the Blue Mountains above Weston, Oregon.

"Hudson Bay Old White Winter" English Lammas Wheat

Governor I. I. Stevens, in his 1854 journal, unwittingly helped locate HBC Farm when he wrote, "Some eighteen or twenty miles up the Walla Walla River is a so-called farm, on which there are two small hovels, each consisting of a single room, occupied by a servant and Indian employed as herdsman. There was formerly a dam at this place for irrigation, but it is broken down." "On the ground logic" contends that the dam (diversion) Stevens mentioned is the same place the Williams Brothers Hudson Bay Farm diverts water from Schwartz Creek today. The diversion is on a northward bend of the creek, has an 1874 water right, and is some 400 yards west of Goodman's "old" farmhouse. This diversion point allows water to run down a 1% grade and across 135 acres of flat land to Pine Creek. For irrigation, this is an ideal setup, especially if you were working with 1820s tools. Tom Williams knows of several other diversion points on Schwartz Creek. The dam at the 1874 water right is the only one that makes sense. The cold, clear water from Schwartz Creek could have easily supported a small settlement, provided water for stock and allowed precise control of irrigation water to a 60-acre field.

Still missing are the names of those who lived and worked on the historic HBC Farm. All the available HBC employee records for Fort Nez Percés staff make no distinction between those assigned to the fort, farm, and gardens. The 1872 Bergevin Frenchtown map does not include Métis cabins at the Hudson's Bay Farm. Some of the employees there may have been Hawaiians who were familiar with growing things, hired Indians who tended the herds, or Métis who "commuted" from Frenchtown. Sharecroppers, if there were any, were not mentioned in any HBC reports.

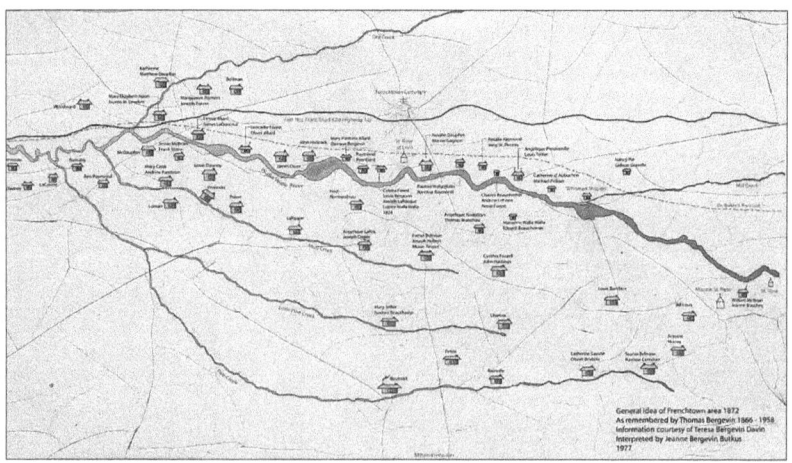

Frenchtown Métis Settler Map
Courtesy Historic Frenchtown Foundation

We do have some limited information on dwellings at the farm from the Frazier Farmstead Museum Collection in nearby Milton-Freewater:

"There was a meadow with springs rising in it and a steep bank close by, where dugouts were constructed for winter shelter. This was the purpose of the settlement—a place to spend the winter—and it was an ideal place." During the 1862 trial over depredation payments to the Hudson's Bay Company it was noted in the proceedings some of the farm's derelict buildings were still standing. "Document A" from *Hudson's Bay Company vs. The United States* inventories the old farm's assets: "1 dwelling house, 20x15; 1 dairy, built of hewn logs 20x15; 7 M fence rails; and 30 acres cultivated land." A 1930s *Walla Walla Union Bulletin* article contains testimony from several "old timers" who re-member the fallen-in buildings of the Hudson's Bay Farm.

The buildings may be gone, but the legacy remains. Historian Richard Scheuerman recently found USDA documentation of a soft white winter wheat descended from the seed Governor Simpson left during his travels to the region in 1824. With help from the Washington State University Crop Sciences Department, he tracked down what was known regionally as "Hudson Bay wheat" or "Old White Winter." In

**Pambrun Ranch Harvest Crew (c. 1914)
on the Umatilla Indian Reservation
Sam Pambrun Collection**

England the variety was known as White Lammas since it was commonly harvested on Lammas Day, August 1. A field of this historic grain was still growing in the Willamette Valley in 1914 near the small community of Belleville when a USDA plant collector happened on it and saved a sample.

WILLIAMS HUDSON BAY FARM

Today brothers Ray and Tom Williams operate a large, diversified farm at the site of the historic Hudson's Bay Company Farm and retain the name for their enterprise. They recently placed three hundred acres of their Hudson Bay Farm in an organic agricultural conservation easement known as the PCC (Puget Consumers Co-op) Farmland Trust. The purpose of this easement is to conserve the soil, protect the environment and preserve the land for future generations. In this way the legacy continues.

PART II

TIME AND TRUTH

Lee Moorhouse, Hoosis Mox Mox
(Snake River–Palouse Chief Husis Maksmaks, c. 1910)
Támastslikt Cultural Institute

DECOLONIZING PALOUSE HISTORY: ORAL HISTORY OF ANDREW GEORGE AND MARY JIM

Clifford E. Trafzer
and Richard D. Scheuerman

O ral history of tribal people of the Columbia Plateau includes both old and new narrations. Tribal histories begin with oral accounts carefully preserved across time, accounts that are central elements of scholarly work designed to deconstruct the "textbook" version of the past by honoring the actual knowledge and memories of tribal elders and reservation scholars. Through the spoken word, tribal histories offer significant and often untapped knowledge of Indigenous pasts. These accounts may contradict the written words of historical participants and modern scholars. Oral histories are the first histories found in the Western Hemisphere, and they are not "fish tales that grow with the telling."[1]

The words of tribal elders and scholars have an important place within the academy, one dismissed by too many scholars even up to the not-so-distant past. Much can be learned by taking the time to earn the trust of tribal people with knowledge of the past and by learning from them their creation stories, methods of food acquisition, cultural beliefs, change of values over time, and methods of remembering.[2] Tribal elders may sing, tell stories without endings, or invite researchers to special places within the native universe. Sometimes their silence tests the willingness of outsiders to be courteously patient, listen carefully, and not speak. Tribal elders have many ways of conveying knowledge and ways of knowing, thinking, and analyzing the past and present.[3]

To illustrate the significance of oral history, we share our experiences among two elders in particular: Andrew George and Mary Jim. Both have now walked on, both were of *Naxiyamtáma* (Snake River-Palouse) descent, and both born in the first decade of the twentieth century.[4] They were raised along the lower Snake River among their people who lived roughly from present-day Lewiston, Idaho, to Pasco, Washington. Andrew George was born about 1900 in the vicinity of the Washington-Idaho border and Mary Jim was born ten years later at *Samyúya*, a village on the Snake River about a dozen miles upstream from its confluence with the Columbia.[5] Their families had much in common and they grew up in the old way, led by strong parents and village leaders. Their relatives had fought against the United States Army and civilian volunteers during the Plateau Indian Wars of the 1850s. Their families worshiped in the way of the *Washani* faith and Indian Shaker Church. They participated in *Washat* ceremonies, also known as the Seven Drums Religion.

Their families still lived by hunting, fishing, and gathering at that time. Mary and Andrew learned the tenets of *tamánwit*, the sacred laws of Plateau people, when they were young. They learned about important geography and places, about tribal economics, plant life, animals, ceremony, and *Washat*. Through the oral tradition, elders taught them how to act correctly in accordance with tribal social, spiritual, and cultural rules, including how to treat others. Whenever adults spoke, Andrew and Mary learned to be silent, listen, and learn, not speaking unless asked to do so. A violation might mean a visit from the Whip

Man who would punish children with a switch, or the threat of a visit from the Witch Woman.[6]

Stories were repeated to them many times year round, but especially in the winter months. As they grew older, they would be asked to repeat stories, like "Why Coyote Made the Palouse Hills" and "How Palouse Falls Was Created," receiving corrections and tempered praise until telling them correctly. Through the oral tradition, they learned this Indigenous way of knowing, remembering, and teaching.[7] Yakama elder and author Virginia Beavert (Tuxámshish) explains storytelling enabled each generation to teach the next ones in the future.[8]

Just as these children did, scholars and authors can benefit from sitting quietly while master teachers inform them of tribal history. Their retelling in journal and book drafts of their work should be checked with their Indigenous teachers before publishing. In this way, elders can respond to how these scholars have framed their interpretations. Sharing information in this way advances trust and knowledge.[9] Authors might also consider providing their teachers, and tribal libraries, archives and cultural centers, with documents, photographs, maps, and other useful findings from their vetted research.

Andrew George

By the 1960s, Andrew had earned a reputation as a highly regarded holy man and healer, a spiritual leader of the *Washat*. He was a prominent *twáti*, or holy man, and tribal members across the Northwest knew of him and his power. He was related to several past Indigenous leaders, including famous chiefs of the nineteenth century like Tílqawayks (Tilcoax) and Xalish Wáshumki (Wolf Necklace).[10]

But Andrew was an elusive man, always traveling from reservation to reservation and from one native community to another. For over three years, we sought to meet and consult him about a study of the Palouse people. Wherever we traveled, we were told about him but could never find him. He was like a phantom.

Andrew George (c. 1985)
Spencer Collection, Tamástslikt Cultural Institute,
Pendleton, Oregon

Finally in the fall of 1980, we did find him. With the help of Carrie Jim, Mary's daughter, we learned he was living with his daughter on the Yakama Reservation in Central Washington.[11] It was November 15, and a darkly gathering sky ushered in cold and wind that portended snow. It was *Sekhlewahl*, "Moon of the Falling Leaves" and winter was definitely in the air.[12] After locating the residence, we knocked and two small girls answered the door. We asked if Andrew George was in and if we could speak to him. The youngsters laughed, ran off, and left the door open. The cold November wind blew into the house and swirled around the door. We wondered if we should leave. Andrew emerged from a hallway to the left, reached out, and brought us into the house where we sat at the kitchen table and where Andrew held us rapt with stories of tribal heritage.

It appeared to us that he had anticipated our arrival and prepared himself to educate us in this native way. Around a kitchen table he related how the Palouse Hills of Eastern Washington and northern Idaho were borne from the mind of *Spilyaí*, Coyote. Andrew explained that the Animal People gathered along *Pik'únen* (lower Snake River) where Coyote envisioned the creation of the Palouse Hills.[13] Coyote created the hills believing their shape would be to his advantage when he challenged other Animals to races, particularly Turtle. Andrew explained that this account and many like them were factual as he had learned the old accounts from trusted tribal elders and family members. "The history of my family and people has been told by my uncles and other elders," Andrew said. "It is written in the ancient rocks."[14] Like his elders before him, he explained his people considered these stories to be sacred truths, not fairy tales.[15]

Academics may be surprised by the Indigenous methodology of learning and teaching oral history by storytelling, that information is known through the means of ancient oral narratives. According to the Palouse Hills story, Turtle outsmarted Coyote, using clever forethought and intelligence to win the race.[16] Listeners learn lessons, and that Coyote's act of creation made the beautiful undulating hills that characterize much of Eastern Washington, western Idaho, and northeastern Oregon. As Andrew showed, Indigenous history explains the landscape and special places within the natural environment.[17]

Native American history like this is just waiting for researchers to enter and acquire it. For outsiders, a new way of seeing, thinking, and experiencing the past and present is possible. The rolling Palouse Hills and surrounding landscapes, like the age-old messages recorded on its very rocks, are a reminder that the Animal People inhabited earth before humans arrived.[18] Through stories going back to the flood age, the Palouse believe they were the first humans to live in this part of the Inland Northwest. They were, in the words of Snake River-Palouse elder Atilapum, "first in this land."[19]

During that first interview with Andrew, he spoke and reflected on many things and said that he felt sorry for university biologists and agricultural scientists "because they have never spoken with plants and animals, and they have never heard their songs. I have seen things they have never seen and heard things they may never hear. I have heard their songs and stories."[20]

Many tribal elders and scholars have a unique relationship with their cultural landscapes, which includes experiential, spiritual, and scientific knowledge of plants, places, animals, and water courses. They know of places of power within their home environments, where energy concentrates causing dangerous locations that must be respected, including Rock Lake, which was once inhabited by a fearsome monster.[21]

Listening with an open mind is a powerful learning tool, especially with tribal guides at places like former village sites, unmarked cemeteries, battle grounds, and places where spirits or gods interacted with each other, the environment, and human beings.[22] Andrew spoke of his early life in the village of *Palus* located at the confluence of the Snake and Palouse Rivers. The village was located downstream of Palouse Falls in the rugged canyon which Giant Beaver carved out in the time of the Animal People, creating one large and several smaller falls.[23] According to Snake River-Palouse elder Gordon Fisher, *Palus* received its name from a Sahaptin word, *Ehpelútpa*, which means "Above the Water," a reference to the petrified heart of Beaver after he had clawed his way down the Palouse River.[24] According to the ancient story, warriors killed Beaver at the Palouse's junction with the Snake, where his heart petrified into a massive stone outcropping.[25]

Andrew knew of this formation that existed until steamboat officials blew it up to allow vessels to pass through the area safely. Eventually, dams on the Snake flooded the former site of Beaver's heart. Indigenous landmarks, former villages, and burial grounds also disappeared when water behind Lower Monumental Dam inundated the area. The rising water covered the old village site, the place where horses had crossed the Snake from the south to the north, and the base of the canyon leading to the "horse grazing pastures" north of the river on the plateau above. Andrew explained that the story of Giant Beaver was true, as he had seen his claw marks on the cliffs above the falls. The rocks spoke the truth, he said. Though *Ehpelútpa* is gone, this site and others remain significant to native people: landmarks important and sacred within the Palouse landscape.[26]

Andrew felt researchers should know more about the many familial ties between Plateau tribes like the Nez Perce, Cayuse, Wanapum, Yakama, Walla Walla, Umatilla, and other peoples of the greater Northwest including Sahaptin-, Interior Salishan-, and Chinookan-speaking peoples. All of these tribes intermingled, intermarried, and all shared concerns about the rapid encroachment of non-natives. Most families had relatives among other tribes of the Northwest, including the family of Chief Red Heart.[27]

Andrew's father was a well-known Palouse man named Hay-hay-tah, also known as Smith L. George. His mother was Julia Redheart Johnson of the Nez Perce Chief Redheart Band. Andrew explained that his mother and her family had fought the United States Army and volunteer settler soldiers during the Nez Perce War of 1877, though he said his mother and her family rarely spoke about the war.[28] When they did, he said, they wept remembering their hardships in *Eekish Pah*, the "Hot Place," or Indian Territory in present-day Kansas and Oklahoma. They wept, he said, for the graves of loved ones left at Fort Leavenworth, Kansas, and the Quapaw Agency and the Ponca Reservation of Indian Territory (present-day Oklahoma).

Julia's parents were Palouse elders Ipnamatwekin and Ahnanemart (Dick and Fannie Johnson).[29] Following the Nez Perce War, Julia, her parents, and siblings, underwent forced removal to *Eekish Pah*.[30] With orders from General William T. Sherman, the Army exiled Palouse, Cayuse, and Nez Perce people to Indian Territory Andrew knew that while in *Eekish Pah*, the people often died of starvation and exposure, as well as malaria, influenza, and other diseases.[31] They also suffered widespread anomie and general depression due to their deprivations and separation from their Northwest homes. The Army turned uncooperative prisoners over to agents of the Indian Office. Government bureaucrats moved these prisoners of war to the Quapaw Agency, then to the newly formed Ponca Agency where they continued to suffer and feel forsaken. Andrew's people remained on the Ponca Reservation until 1885 when the government allowed them to return to the Northwest.[32] Government agents sent some of the people to the Nez Perce Reservation in Idaho and others to the Colville Reservation at Nespelum, Washington where many of their descendants live today.[33]

When Andrew's people returned to the Northwest, his grandparents and mother lived on a reservation until the family slipped away and quietly returned to *Palus*. Until the first years of the twentieth century, some Palouse families lived peacefully there and elsewhere along the rivers. It was during this time, around 1900, that Andrew was born.[34] Knowing this family history helps explain his chosen path and how important to him was his gift of healing given by the spirit world. Possessing a strong *tah* or spiritual power, Andrew became a *twáti* and an influential man of spiritual authority. In the tradition of Plateau people, it was not proper to divulge the nature of this power, although it gave him a special ability to help and heal others.[35] He would call upon it often during his entire life.

Unfortunately, the villagers could not overcome another government-forced removal from their ancient river homes. When Andrew was a boy, soldiers and government officials invaded *Palus*. They removed all the inhabitants, forcing them to board a steamboat and abandon their ancient village. If tribal leaders had warned of the invasion and planned removal, young Andrew did not know of it.[36] All were confused and traumatized to be severed again from land upon which, for so many generations, they had moved like the wind to hunt, fish, gather, and conduct ceremonies. Land in which lay the bones of ancestors. They were taken to Lapwai, Idaho, where agents enrolled them on the Nez Perce Reservation.[37]

Andrew said that his family's forced removal from their home and the steamboat trip to Lapwai seemed like a dream, with images of the removal flickering "like a vision of the way things were."[38] Some years later, he asked his elders if his memory was a dream or reality. They confirmed that it was correct. Unfortunately it was an all too common experience across North America as the government forced tribes from their villages and homelands, stealing their lands and resources to benefit settlers and development.[39] Many students today know of the forced removal of the Cherokee, Choctaw, Chickasaw, Seminole, and Muscogee to reservations and boarding schools.[40] Social studies and history textbook often mention these tribes. However, little is known by non-natives about the many other forced removals of Indigenous people by federal, state, and local governments, not to mention ad hoc committees of settlers. Inland Northwest tribes lost their homes and access to many important cultural places their people had known for generations and still honor.[41]

Though they now lived at the Nez Perce Reservation at Lapwai, Andrew and his people would leave there to roam as before and Andrew traveled a great deal as a child and young man. In addition to moving between fishing, hunting, and gathering areas, he spent time living on the Colville Reservation. At other times, he lived on the Umatilla and Spokane Reservations. Wherever he lived, on a reservation or special sites on the Plateau, he and his family remained independent and self-reliant.[42] At Lapwai, Nespelem, Pendleton, Andrew spent considerable time learning from elders. Like worthy contemporary scholars learning in Indigenous ways, Andrew listened, absorbed, and applied his knowledge in the service of others.[43]

As he traveled he also learned about the land and places. He explained that he and his family lived "all over the place—Snake River, Nez Perce, Spokane."[44] While in the pursuit of hunting, fishing, and gathering, he listened and learned. At night while camping, the people would gather near a fire where adults would tell ancient stories.

Andrew learned, he says, "how the land was made and how salmon came to the rivers. It was all the Creator's plan, just like it says in the Bible."[45]

> We heard the stories over and over again and the elders had us repeat them. . . . Our history is our stories, and you can see them in the rocks.[46] [The people commonly believed that the Creator] fashioned their images in the petroglyphs along the Snake River and at places like Priest Rapids on the Middle Columbia as instructions for the people. Those stones are so sacred, so we did not touch them.[47]

Recognizing his innate ability to tap into power within himself, tribal ceremonial leaders and healers guided him in his future work as a *twáti*.[48] Andrew George harnessed the healing spirits to learn about his environment and people. Power came to him in visions or dreams. He learned songs given him by the spirit world. He used his powers to counsel and heal others. In time and with guidance from his elders, Andrew grew into the role of a *twáti*,[49] a spiritual leader, and the spirit world enhanced his power to help, counsel, and heal others.[50]

Andrew also used his spiritual powers and abilities to conduct ceremonies in the old way, concentrating power for the well-being of the people. Until his death, Andrew was among the most respected and celebrated Indian doctors in the Northwest. Unlike Western medical doctors who attend schools of medicine, Native American healers receive special gifts from the spirit world to do their work, and may have familiars or spirit helpers to call upon for assistance, often through unique songs.[51]

Andrew George once healed Nez Perce scholar Josiah Pinkham and his sister after an incident which nearly cost them their lives. In July 2008, Josiah told the story at a consultation about a proposed exhibit at the National Cowboy and Western Heritage Museum. Curators were planning an exhibit on the Palouse, Nez Perce, and Cayuse exiles in Indian Territory. One evening, Andrew's name came up,[52] and Josiah said, "that old man . . . once healed me and my sister."[53]

He explained that when he and she were in high school, they drove from Lapwai to the Yakama Reservation to play in a basketball tournament. They drove home late that same night and in the early morning hours, while driving over the bridge heading into Lapwai, a "force" took control of the steering wheel, turning the vehicle into the Clearwater River. As the car sank into the swiftly flowing water, Josiah and his sister barely escaped with their lives. After swimming to shore, they were hospitalized and ultimately released.[54] Although medical doctors announced they were fine physically, however, their mother was not convinced. She believed someone had bewitched her children. Without telling them, she invited Andrew to doctor them. Josiah said one day they returned home from school to find Andrew sitting in their house. Upon seeing them, Andrew peered at the empty space behind them, as if something or someone was following them. Andrew blew hot water on them and put his arms around them, slapping their bodies, driving the entity out. He cleansed them, Josiah said, using his spiritual power, pure water, and the physical actions of his hands and arms to drive the negative force from their bodies. The dangerous entity could not stand against Andrew's positive power and they were freed.[55]

Carrie Jim Schuster remembers Andrew as "a Longhouse spiritual leader" who also became "a leader in the All-Tribes Church." According to Carrie, Andrew "was a disciplinarian but never needed to execute his power. Everyone respected him."[56]

Andrew's healing nature and his awareness of natural balances and the lessons of history informed his concern about numerous issues, including the dwindling number of salmon and their right to survive. He said that not only did Native Americans have natural fishing rights based on the Creator's gifts, but that fish also have rights, and humans should not diminish this natural resource, especially salmon. For many years, tribal people have fought for their right to fish at "all usual and accustomed fishing places . . . in common with citizens," language of several treaties of the Northwest.[57] During the 1970s and

1980s, Andrew closely followed legal issues arising over fishing, including overfishing and dams.

As he often did to help illustrate imbalances and threats to the native laws of *tamánwit*, Andrew offered two ancient accounts. The first was about how salmon gained power to preserve their lives and remind humans not to overfish.[58]

According to Andrew's account, the Salmon People were alarmed that early peoples were catching and taking far more salmon than they needed to eat and trade. To remedy the problem, Salmon Chief traveled up Snake River to find Rattlesnake and obtain some of his poison. Humans feared Rattlesnake, so Salmon Chief set out to acquire some of Rattlesnake's power. Salmon Chief traveled the river until he found Rattlesnake sunning himself on a large boulder. Salmon Chief approached and explained that humans were taking too many fish, and that he wanted to obtain some of Rattlesnake's poison. When Rattlesnake refused to share his poison, Salmon Chief responded by hitting Rattlesnake on the head with his mighty tail. Four times Salmon Chief asked Rattlesnake for his poison. Four times Rattlesnake refused to share it. After beating the dangerous snake on the head the fifth time, Rattlesnake grudgingly gave Salmon Chief some of his poison, which the chief shared with all Salmon People.[59] To this day, salmon have a small portion of Rattlesnake's power, which they hold in their mouths to bite Indigenous fishers, reminding them not to overfish.[60]

In the second story, Andrew explained that as children they learned how salmon came to some rivers and not others.[61] The story involves Five Monster Sisters called the *Tah Tah Kleah* who settled on the lower *Nch'i-Wána* ("Big Water") or the Columbia River. The sisters broke with *tamánwit* by building a dam on the Columbia to hold back the salmon. The greedy monsters thought only of themselves and not about the salmon that had to spawn upriver or about the people upriver including Grizzly Bear, Cougar, Raccoon, Black Bear, Badger, and others that depended on the fish to survive. The Animal People held council.

Someone, they realized, had to break the fish dam. No one volunteered except Coyote, periodically a protector, creator, and clever instigator. Using forethought and intelligence to break the fish dam, he would become a hero.[62]

Coyote outwitted the *Tah Tah Kleah* and broke the dam with five digging sticks, then led the Salmon up the Columbia River and its tributaries into the Inland Northwest. Coyote became a Salmon Chief as his decisions established laws about which rivers the salmon would use to spawn. If the Animal People were kind to Coyote, giving him food and wives, he allowed the salmon to enter their rivers and pass alongside their villages. If they were stingy, Coyote would not allow the salmon to travel past their villages. Those living on the banks of the Snake River were generous to Coyote, so he allowed the salmon to travel near to their villages, including *Kwásis, Tyáwtas, Tásiwks, Samyúya, Shapanúk, Palús, Alamótin,* and *Wawáwi.* Eventually the Palouse people took advantage of Coyote's gift and established their villages in the same places on the lower Snake. The salmon sustained them until the government violated *tamánwit* by building dams. In breaking this sacred law of creation, dams significantly reduced the number of salmon alive today and have threatened their future.[63]

In accordance with the laws of creation, rivers, streams, and creeks should flow freely through the landscape; it is against nature's law to dam them. "Damning up the rivers is just like cutting off the blood of your arm or leg," he explained. "You can live for a while without some parts of your body, but by cutting off the flow, sooner or later you'll die." According to Andrew, "That's how it is with the river and salmon."[64]

Mary Jim

Xínstanik or Mary Jim Chapman, another respected Palouse tribal elder, knew these legends and told them as well as stories of her life, through the oral tradition.[65] In 1975, Richard Scheuerman met Mary through Wanapum elder and *Washat* leader, Rex Buck, Sr.[66] Richard had learned about Mary by reading her story about growing up traveling to early root grounds on horseback, dragging a travois of tipi poles in "Echo Mountains at Palouse [Falls]." The story was one of several in a classic collection edited by Yakama elder Virginia Beavert (Tuxámshish) called *Anakú Iwachá: Yakama Legends and Stories.*[67] This is a compilation of traditional oral narratives and ancient legends told by knowledgeable tribal elders.[68] Mary's essay interested Richard who had grown up on a farm in the heart of Palouse country, not far from a former Palouse village. He had spent considerable time researching the Snake River-Palouse people.[69]

Mary Jim Chapman Crafting a Rootbag (1977)
Spencer Collection, Tamástslikt Cultural Institute
Pendleton, Oregon

Mary invited him to her home on the Yakama Reservation where she began to tell him about her life over what would be the course of several oral history interviews. Two years later, Scheuerman took Clifford Trafzer along to meet and learn from her too.[70] Over the following years, Mary Jim contributed significantly to the preservation of knowledge about Palouse people and Indigenous life on the Columbia Plateau during the twentieth century. She was invaluable to the research published in our 1986 book *Renegade Tribe: The Palouse Indians and the Invasion of the Inland Pacific Northwest*.[71]

Mary Jim's entire life was guided by a deeply rooted connection to her homeland along the Snake River.[72] She was born in 1910 to the lands of her ancestors in the village of *Samyúya* on the south side of the river. Two generations earlier, soldiers had invaded these lands during the Plateau Indian War in the 1850s. Oregon volunteers under the command of Colonel Thomas Cornelius drove Palouse families from the river in an aggressive military action. Her grandfather, Fishhook Jim, escaped but his brother, Estamlóot was only about ten years old and could not get away. Colonel Cornelius captured the boy and handed him over to missionaries probably at St. Rose Mission, located about ten miles west of present-day Walla Walla. Estamlóot attended Catholic school, learned English, and came to be called "Thomash" by his people, perhaps a form of "Thomas" after Cornelius.[73] As a young man, Thomash returned to the Snake River where he became a respected chief, spokesman, and man of spiritual power.[74]

According to Mary Jim, when the government later tried to force Thomash and his people onto a reservation, he spoke for them all, saying, "We don't want to leave this fishing place; we don't want to leave this graveyard; we don't want to leave. How would we keep our horses?"[75] As a result of his leadership, the Palouse living on the lower Snake did not immediately move to a reservation and remained at their villages where they kept vast herds of horses. Each family had horses, which were wealth to them; they bred high quality animals that grazed on the bunch grass of the Columbia Plateau. Through selective breeding, they raised highly prized horses known for their strength, endurance, and intelligence.[76]

Mary Jim learned to ride at the same time she learned to walk, she said.[77] In her youth, she and her people routinely traveled across the Plateau on horseback. In *Wosihtash*, "Moving Out Time" (March and April), men and boys rounded up the horses that had grazed on winter bunchgrass,[78] breaking them in after they had run free during the winter. Mary and the other girls and the women would prepare travois and pack horses for traveling to early root grounds, often north to Soap Lake.[79] There they camped with other families, not just Palouse, but Yakama, Colville, Warm Springs, Coeur d'Alene, Spokane, and Nez Perce.[80]

With a *kapon* or digging stick, families dug *sk'okul*, *xmass*, and other roots.[81] For weeks, people camped together in their tents and tipis while moving across the Plateau gathering nutritious roots and reuniting with other native families that they knew. They also visited with friendly White residents including Yakima Valley rancher L. V. McWhorter, Hooper businessman Maurice McGregor, Ephrata farmer Cull White, Okanogan judge William Brown, and Dayton rancher Sherman Pettyjohn. These men and several women were friends to Native Americans, allowing them to cross their lands, to hunt, gather, and camp on their private property—lands that had once been used exclusively by Indigenous people.

When it was learned that salmon were swimming upstream in the Columbia, the travelers would pack their belongings and move on to their fishing areas, each family having their own spot where they had natural fishing rights in accordance with *tamánwit*.[82] This phase of the year was called *Koiyaahl*, "Moon of the Summer Salmon," when the people caught and dried fish (chiefly salmon) and eels for winter use. In October, they moved on to hunt for game in a time they called *Hopelul* (Moon When Tamarack Turn Yellow). In the mountains, they killed and dressed deer, elk, and other animals as well as preserving meat for the winter. They picked berries to dry and store as well. As the weather turned cold, they returned to their homes along the Snake to store the meat, repair their A-framed tule-mat lodges, gather wood, and prepare for winter.[83]

This seasonal round of traveling to food sources, gathering roots, picking berries, fishing, and hunting had been their way of life for countless centuries. It was the natural rhythm of survival and included showing gratitude to the earth and the Creator for their gifts. These foods connected the people with each other and to the spirit world. Mary, her family, and all the Plateau tribes had a deep and abiding association with salmon as well as game animals, roots, and berries, and these remain the sacred foods of Snake River-Palouse people and all their Plateau neighbors.[84]

As an element of *tamánwit*, throughout the year, the people gave thanks for their native foods in ceremonies. First Foods Ceremonies are at once ancient and contemporary, tying the past to present generations. The Plateau people remember, honor, and thank the foods for their existence. At the same time, they thank the Creator for providing these sacred foods significant to their physical, mental, and spiritual health.[85]

As a young woman from a leadership family, Mary Jim organized, prepared, and participated in First Food Ceremonies. She successfully passed along her deep belief in and adherence to these thanksgiving ceremonies to her community. During the second half of the twentieth century, Mary initiated a yearly gathering of Palouse and other tribal people at Fishhook Park on the Snake River. Usually in May, Mary, her family, and others would meet at the park for a few days of celebration which included a First Foods Ceremony. The First Foods Ceremony cements the spiritual ties of the people with plants, animals, and water that had sustained the lives of Plateau people since the time of creation. The ceremonies are central to *Washat* beliefs, and have been practiced since time immemorial through the *Washani* faith.[86]

Andrew George explained that the ceremonies conducted around the sacred foods taught children to respect the Creator's gifts and "learn the sacred ways that give life."[87] Mary Jim expressed the same sentiment. "The First Foods Feast shows the Creator's way," she said.

> *"Start with water (kús), then the chiefs of the creatures: salmon [nú-sux] for fish and venison [deer/yámas] for animals, then the plants [bitterroot/piyáxi] and fruits [huckleberries/wíwinu]. We do this each season. The land was our religion; given to us by the Creator. The earth is our Mother because it provides all food. Imepship [the Great Spirit] placed us on our Imephsha [Earth Mother] who gives us roots and berries. The sacred foods share the earth with us."*[88]

Washat ceremonies are never "performed." They are not entertainment, and no audience exists, only participants. During *Washat* ceremonies each person drinks water and eats foods as sacred links between the Creator, the foods, and the participant.[89] Diligent, respectful researchers might earn the right to participate in these holy ceremonies as a way of learning and sharing those things that tribal consultants feel can be shared with others. Such a privilege might take time, but once admitted into the ceremonial circle, researchers must act in a trusted manner, sharing the sacred foods with elders and children alike. If researchers write about the ceremony, they must inform others accurately, appropriately, and in consultation with their tribal hosts.

Indigenous peoples throughout the native universe of the Western Hemisphere conduct First Foods Ceremonies—not just the people of the Columbia Plateau. Carrie Jim explains that they provide a focused means to "follow the Creator's way by honoring sacred foods"[90] throughout the native universe, through ceremony, song, and story.[91]

Tribal people have origin accounts of all foods or how humans began eating various plants and animals. The significance of foods so important that the Smithsonian's National Museum of the American Indian offers a dining service featuring foods from many different

Indigenous peoples. Foods known to tribes and regions offer a pathway of understanding that addresses history, culture, society, and religion. Partaking of these foods in fellowship with tribal people offers lessons important to understanding and representing others and enlarges ways of thinking about the past and present. Foods are given a special place in Indigenous cultures and honoring them contributes greatly to the mental, physical, and spiritual well-being of tribal people.[92]

In addition to their annual hunting and gathering cycle, Mary Jim's family did some seasonal farm work to earn cash to buy sugar, coffee, flour, and other items they enjoyed but could not find naturally on the land. During the early twentieth century, many worked as farm laborers picking hops or fruit for cash, but by and large, they lived off the land.[93]

When she was of age, Mary married Alex Jesse Chapman and they began their family. Alex was an accomplished singer and musician, trained by his own people and teachers at Chemawa Indian School in Salem, Oregon.[94] Mary, Alex, and their children remained living along the Snake River near the graves of their loved ones for many years, in a tent home constructed of canvas, boards, plywood, and ropes.[95] They followed their ancestors' cyclical hunting and gathering patterns and worked on farms as needed to get by.

One year during the 1950s while picking strawberries near Pasco, a worker told Mary that someone had set up a tent on *Nch'i-'imá* or "Big Island" on the Snake. In preparation for the building of Ice Harbor Dam, the Army Corps of Engineers had contracted archaeologists to conduct the Mid-Columbia Archaeological Survey. These archaeology crews were digging in the Indigenous cemetery where Mary's mother, father, brothers, and grandfather were buried.[96] Despite any outcry, they ultimately excavated many graves along the river, including Big Island.[97]

In 1959, Richard Daugherty and Roderick Sprague published *Archaeological Excavations in the Ice Harbor Reservoir*, which detailed excavations and exhumation of Palouse ancestors.[98] During burial excavations on Big Island, Mary and her daughters, Carrie and Anna, protested the desecration of their family graves. Mary's cousin Charlie Jim paddled a canoe to the island to protest the theft but was turned back forcefully. The remains of Mary's grandfather, Fishhook Jim, who had been buried in a canoe, were also taken.[99] University archaeologists ignored their protests.[100]

Despite the construction of Ice Harbor Dam and eventual flooding of her home in 1959, Mary could not be coaxed off her land. She steadfastly remained, tied to her past and spiritual beliefs. Mary remembered "the Law" (police officers, sheriff's deputies, and others) eventually descending on her small but defiant family. They were forced into vehicles and driven to the Yakama Reservation to live, but neither the federal government nor the Yakama tribal government provided them with land, housing, or any other assistance. Fortunately, their friends and relatives took them in.[101] During the years that followed, Mary and her family tried many times to return to their homeland. She often "called for our land" as, she felt, it called to her and as the river sang to her.[102] She prayed for the rest of her life to the Creator to intervene so young people could have their "background" and fishing rights.[103]

The desire of Palouse families to live on the Snake River has a soul-deep grounding, and is connected to unseverable, sacred ties to their burial grounds. *Tamánwit* included the obligation of caring for and protecting burial places of ancestors, and bones were not to be disturbed, much less desecrated or removed.[104] Mary felt she had failed. She could never reconcile the loss. "I respect the dead," she said, "because they came here first and lived here. God put them here to live and they had the land and everything, all kinds of food."[105] Her elders had taught her to care for and protect the bones of her ancestors, her grandparents and her parents. And because of the dam, "My mother and grandmother are under water, and my brothers and father are under that water," she said.[106]

As reservation scholar Wilson Wewa explained, many Snake River-Palouse ancestors languished "for years in drawers and boxes."

Aside from the unforgivable injury to the dead, disturbing graves could result in negative consequences in nature, including fires, earthquakes, and other natural disasters, and even cause illnesses, accidents, and sicknesses in the minds and bodies of the living.[107] They believe that the dead have the power to punish the living for disturbances and desecrations.[108]

For many years, Native Americans fought against the excavation of their cemeteries, but their outcry was disregarded by waves of fact-finding archaeologists who persisted in digging up the Indigenous dead for study. Even with the passage of the Native American Graves Protection and Repatriation Act (NAGPRA) of November 1990, the struggle to protect the remains of the dead continues today.

After years of pressure Washington State University and the University of Idaho agreed repatriate the remains of the they had stored in boxes and bags. In November 2006, Native Americans officiated the reburial of these remains that had been locked away for years. Descendants of many Indigenous people and friends met on the banks of the Snake River near Lyons Ferry State Park to rebury their ancestors. After years in storage, they had finally returned home.[109]

For many years, the Jim family tried to have their Snake River homeland restored. Although their homesite was under water, they wanted lands above the waterline where they could live, fish, and raise their children like the generations before them. For forty years and despite obstacles, Mary fought for repatriation, even by addressing the United States Congress. Sadly, the family failed to return home. The Corps of Engineers and the federal government generally did nothing to support the Palouse effort to reclaim even a minuscule portion of their former homelands. Mary Jim died in 2000, but her dream of returning to the Snake River still lives on in her daughter Carrie Jim Schuster, and granddaughter Ione I. Jones, who continue the effort to return to the river. The Snake River still calls them. The spirits of their *Naxiyamtáma* relatives still call them.

During her life, Mary Jim began the tradition of returning to the Snake River each year to honor ancestors, to celebrate their heritage through Seven Drums songs and ceremonies, and to share sacred foods. Now when the families meet at Fishhook Jim Park each spring, individuals speak from their hearts and cry in remembrance. At these times, families give their children native names, and adults take the names of respected ancestors, promising to live a worthy life. Everyone shares in gift-giving. Most of all, everyone leaves the gatherings with a full heart, new knowledge, and a connectedness to their culture through these special rites and rituals. Carrie Jim sums up her thoughts saying, "Through the courage and faith of our elders like my mother we made a new life, but our hearts are still back home, and we return every year."[110]

Fishhook Jim Indian Homestead Location along the Snake River
Authors' Collection

In the fall of 2017, we visited the site of Mary Jim's Snake River home. With photographs in hand, we found the family's former home-place. We stood on a bluff on the south side of the river looking down into the dark water where the Jim family had lived. Mary's home, swimming places, children's playground, fishing sites, and drying racks were no more. Whenever Mary Jim spoke of this place, she wept. We sat on the basalt edge of a plateau overlooking the Snake River quietly interacting with the land, light, sound, and sky, and were moved by these losses. Between the cry of a hawk above us and the sound of the water flowing by below, a profound silence prevailed. The spirits of the *Naxiyamtáma* were there.

The government had taken Mary's and Andrew's homes on the Snake River, sacred places the Creator had given them. But the government had silenced neither Mary and Andrew nor their people. Through the oral tradition, their ancient way of knowing, they both have passed along the essence of the Snake River-Palouse history and culture to adults and children alike. As Carrie explains, "the most important legacy a parent, grandparent, or elder can provide for children is appreciation of their heritage."[111] These legacies live on through the words of tribal elders and scholars who know the stories.

NOTES

[1] Reader's Report II for *Renegade Tribe: The Palouse Indians and the Invasion of the Inland Pacific Northwest*, University of Oklahoma Press, 1984, Authors' Collections. An editor told Trafzer to follow the instructions of the reviewer or the press was not interested in the book manuscript. We withdrew from the contract with the University of Oklahoma Press, took the manuscript to Washington State University, and published the book. In 1986, *Renegade Tribe* won an unsolicited book award for nonfiction. We were surprised that some university presses were not interested in supporting the use of tribal oral histories.

[2] To explore more about the Indigenous universe of the Western Hemisphere, see Gerald McMaster and Clifford E. Trafzer, eds., *Native University: Voices of Indian America* (Washington, D.C.: Smithsonian National Museum of the American Indian and National Geographic Society, 2004), 13-71.

[3] This is an example of patience involved in conducting oral histories with tribal elders. Trafzer once had an invitation to interview a tribal elder living on his reservation and made arrangements four different times to meet with him. To interview this tribal elder, Trafzer traveled over four hundred miles round trip each time to conduct the interview. After arriving at his home, the elder or his wife canceled the interview for a future date. On the fourth attempt, Trafzer conducted the interview for a few hours. Researchers must be persistent and patient with elders agreeing to share an oral interview. In this case, the tribal elder became a friend who shared sacred knowledge, which he asked Trafzer to preserve for the benefit of tribal members. He wanted "everyone" to know. He walked on in 2016, a few months after providing his last interview. Subsequently, Trafzer shared the interview with the elder's wife, family, and museum director of the Colorado River Indian Tribes.

[4] Richard D. Scheuerman and Clifford E. Trafzer, *River Song: Naxiyamtáma (Snake River-Palouse) Oral Traditions from Mary Jim, Andrew George, Gordon Fisher, and Emily Peone* (Pullman: Washington State University Press, 2015), 1. The term *Naxiyamtáma* is associated with the Indigenous people inhabiting the lower Snake River from Lewiston, Idaho, to Pasco, Washington.

[5] Andrew George was of Palouse, Nez Perce, and Spokane heritage. Perhaps his ancestors were from other tribes but these three tribes he claimed as his heritage.

[6] Carrie Jim, now in her late 70s, learned correct behavior from her mother and uncle. She explained that when the family visited Priest Rapids (home of her mother's Wanapum relations) to participate in ceremony, elder women cared for the children and expected them to behave correctly. If children acted out, adults punished them. She provides details of her life within her traditional culture in her as yet unpublished manuscript, "*Kukyáma Tamánwit*: The Timeless Snake River-Palouse Law of Life," Authors' Collections.

[7] Oral Interview with Andrew George by Clifford E. Trafzer, Richard D. Scheuerman, and Lee Ann Smith, November 15, 1980, Yakama Reservation, Authors' Collections.

[8] Virginia Beavert, ed., *Anakú Iwachá: Yakama Legends and Stories* (Toppenish, Washington: The Consortium of Johnson O'Malley Region IV, 1974), x-xii.

[9] For nearly fifty years, we have conducted community-based research with tribal elders and reservation scholars from the Inland Pacific Northwest. We have always followed the way of the elders and try to be their students. After preparing a manuscript, we share it with elders in the tribe and never knowingly misrepresent the content of their oral histories. Once we obtain approval, we submit and publish books and articles on the history of tribes and individuals. It is highly significant for scholars to work in collaboration with tribes and tribal people as well as give back to families and tribes.

[10] Scheuerman and Trafzer, *River Song*, 15, 53, 31. Andrew George was related to Tilcoax and his son, Wolf Necklace, two great chiefs of the Inland Pacific Northwest who fought the United States during the Plateau Indian War, 1855-1858. They were considered among the wealthiest native leaders of the region, owning thousands of high-quality horses. During the Plateau War, they lost approximately one thousand horses when Colonel George Wright's troops captured the horses and killed nearly all of them to make an example of them to the native people. For an in-depth examination of the Plateau Indian War, see Trafzer and Scheuerman, *The Snake River-Palouse*, 71-108, 131.

[11] Carrie Jim, a resident of the Yakama Reservation and student of many tribal elders, announced that Andrew was at his daughter's home. She provided directions and said to follow the pavement on a reservation road to the canal road, turning left then right at the yellow pumphouse. She directed us to follow the canal road until we came to three government houses. Andrew

was staying in the third house, a good sign to us since three is a sacred number to Plateau people.

[12] For traditional accounts about how winter came to be in the Inland Northwest, see Clifford E. Trafzer, ed., *Grandmother, Grandfather, and Old World: Tamánwit Ku Súkat and Traditional Native American Narratives from the Columbia Plateau* (East Lansing: Michigan State University Press, 1998), 54-88. For the Palouse names of the months of the year, see Scheuerman and Trafzer, *River Song*, 75-76. Scheuerman, Trafzer, and Lee Ann Smith visited Andrew George on November 15, 1980, on the Yakama Reservation.

[13] For a version of the story, "Why Coyote Made the Palouse Hills," see Scheuerman and Trafzer, *River Song*, 93-94.

[14] Scheuerman and Trafzer, *River Song*, 75.

[15] Reader's Report II for *Renegade Tribe: The Palouse Indians and the Invasion of the Inland Pacific Northwest* (Norman, Oklahoma: University of Oklahoma Press) 1984, Authors' Collection. For an insightful and significant essay on the significance of Plateau Indian oral histories and Indigenous rights, see Andrew H. Fisher, "This I Know from the Old People: Yakama Indian Treaty Rights," *Montana: The Magazine of Western History* 49, No. 1 (Spring 1999), 13-15.

[16] Traditional stories often teach lessons to be emulated. In this case, the story of Turtle defeating Coyote in the foot race teaches us to work with our family and use forethought and intelligence in all human actions.

[17] Scheuerman and Trafzer, *River Song*, 74.

[18] Gilbert Minthorn, "Yamástas," 1930; translation from Sahaptin to English by Morris Swandish of the ancient story about the great flood on the Columbia Plateau, American Philosophical Society, Philadelphia, Pennsylvania.

[19] Ibid.

[20] Scheuerman and Trafzer, *River Song*, 16.

[21] Field Notes by Clifford E. Trafzer and Richard D. Scheuerman, June 6, 2024, Authors' Collections; Fisher, "This I Know from the Old People," 14-15.

[22] In 2016, Palouse elder Carrie Jim Schuster led us on a research trip into the Palouse country. In 2022, she led us on another trip along the Yakima River to Horn Rapids where her family fished salmon while camping at this cultural site. She explained where her family as well as other families camped during the weeks of fishing at these rapids, which are still fished by native men, women, and children. In another part of Indian country, Trafzer spent two years encouraging the local cultural committee to conduct a research project with the Army Corps of Engineers to protect Indigenous historical, cultural, and spiritual sites and landscapes situated on federal lands. After agreeing to the

project, the tribal leadership and committee members took him to "Quechan University." Not an actual physical campus of buildings, their university was the regional cultural landscape that included sacred places, trails, intaglios, village sites, and two major rivers. Researchers will learn much from tribal elders if they are invited into the tribe's university: their traditional cultural landscapes on and off reservations.

23 Scheuerman and Trafzer, *River Song,*105-106.

24 Ibid., 116-118.

25 In the view of Indigenous people, Palouse Falls and the rocks surrounding it are proof of their traditional stories about Beaver and other accounts not referenced in this work. Trafzer and Scheuerman, *The Snake River-Palouse,* xvi, 2, 164.

26 Oral Interview with Andrew George by Clifford E. Trafzer, Richard D. Scheuerman, and Lee Ann Smith, Yakima Reservation, November 15, 1980, Authors' Collections; Scheuerman and Trafzer, *River Song,* 73.

27 L.V. McWhorter, *Yellow Wolf: His Own Story* (Caldwell, Idaho: Caxton Printers, 1940), 104-105, 117, 310-311; Richard Scheuerman has spent fifty years compiling kinship, marriage, births, and deaths of Plateau tribal members; see Richard D. Scheuerman, "Kinship and Marriage Among the Palouse" and "Kamiakin Family History," unpublished manuscript and chart, Authors' Collections, University of California, Riverside.

28 *River Song,* on page 76, see footnotes 1 and 2.

29 In November 2023, we attended a *Washat* celebration at the Longhouse on the Umatilla Reservation where David Wolf and Jeremy Wolf took the names of two prominent relatives of the nineteenth century, Palouse Chiefs Tílqawayks (Tilcoax) and Xalish Washumki (Harlish Wáshimuxsh, Wolf Necklace), who fought as patriots for their people in the Plateau Indian War, 1855-1858. David and Jeremy are related to Andrew George. Umatilla-Palouse elder Nona Pond, daughter of Dr. Ronald Pond, addressed attendees, remembering her Palouse people who once lived in villages along Snake River. She spoke of her people once being led by Hahtálekin and Húsis Kute.

30 Two bands of Palouse joined the Nez Perce during the war, including Chiefs Húsis Kute (Bald Head) and Hahtálekin (also known as Takttsoukt Llppilp, Red Echo). Julia Johnson and her family followed both these Palouse leaders until the Battle of the Big Hole (1877) where soldiers shot and killed Hahtálekin and his son, Five Fogs, during the battle. Julia's family then followed the leadership of Húsis Kute who survived the war and lived out his life on the Colville Reservation.

[31] At Bear Paw, Chief Joseph, with the consent of other leaders, surrendered to Colonel Nelson Miles and General Oliver Howard. The Indians understood this was a conditional surrendered they had negotiated; under terms made in the field, they would winter in Montana and in the spring of 1878, return to Idaho. When word reached Washington, D.C. and William T. Sherman, General of the Army, he reversed the decision made in good faith in Montana. He ordered the Nez Perce, Palouse, and Cayuse to be imprisoned as prisoners of war at Fort Leavenworth, Kansas. Sherman broke the negotiated agreement.

[32] McWhorter, *Yellow Wolf*, 47-51; L. V. McWhorter, *Hear Me, My Chiefs!: Nez Perce History and Legend* (Caldwell, Idaho: The Caxton Printers, 1983), 265, 272, 331-334.

[33] Several works address the Nez Perce War of 1877, including the following list, which is not exhaustive:

- Alvin Josephy, Jr. *The Nez Perce Indians and the Opening of the Northwest* (New Haven: Yale University Press, 1965)
- Trafzer and Scheuerman, *The Snake River-Palouse*, 128-130
- Jerome A Greene, *Nez Perce Summer*, 1877 (Helena: Montana Historical Society Press, 2000)
- Oliver O. Howard, *Nez Perce Joseph* (Boston: Lee and Shepard, 1881)
- Oliver O. Howard, *My Life and Experiences Among Our Hostile Indians* (Hartford, Connecticut: A. D. Worthington & Company, 1907)
- J. Diane Pearson, *The Nez Perces in the Indian Territory: Nimiipuu Survival* (Norman, Oklahoma: University of Oklahoma Press, 2008)
- Clifford E. Trafzer, "The Palouse in Eekish Pah," *American Indian Quarterly* 9, No. 2 (1985), 169-181.

[34] Oral Interview with Andrew George by Clifford E. Trafzer, Richard D. Scheuerman, and Lee Ann Smith, November 15, 1980, Yakama Reservation, Authors' Collections.

[35] Three native people from the Columbia Plateau shared aspects of their *wyakin* or spirit helpers. Texanap was a *Wenatchi* medicine woman. She did not share the source of her power but her daughter, Ida Nason, explained in the film, *Everything Changing, Everything Changing*, that her mother's power as a healer was transferred to her by her father. During Texanap's vision quest, she received power from water bugs, skirting across a small body of water. In

McWhorters book, *Yellow Wolf*, 13, the Nez Perce warrior mentioned part of his power as a warrior, conveyed to him by a Yellow Wolf. His greater power was White Thunder or White Lightning, a source of his *wyakin* that he spoke little about. In the last example, Mourning Dove (Christine Quintasket), a Salish-speaking women of note, revealed her power after white friends pressured her into revealing that her power was a feather flowing through her bloodstream. After sharing this information, Humishuma became ill and ultimately died. As tribal elder Mary Nelson explained to me: "Humishuma, you told too much, told too much." Andrew George was not culturally permitted to share his *wyakin* and carefully guarded his power, which he used to held and heal others.

[36] Trafzer and Scheuerman, *The Snake River-Palouse*, 164.

[37] Ibid.

[38] Ibid.

[39] Ibid.

[40] Beginning in 1879 with the establishment of Carlisle Indian Industrial School in Carlisle, Pennsylvania, the United States began the off-reservation American Indian boarding school system, which included many schools, among them Haskell Institute, Sherman Institute, Bacon, Riverside Indian School, Fort Sill Indian School, Chemawa, Bacone, and many others. The United States created these and other Indian schools to destroy Indigenous cultures, languages, familial attachments, nearly every aspect of traditional Native American life. The boarding and day schools were part of the cultural genocide attempted by the United States against Native Americans and their children. The federal government trained Native Americans to be a useful labor force. The schools changed over time, with far greater native control after the 1960s and the Indigenous civil rights movement. Off-reservation boarding schools changed with time, and the study of the schools is complicated. Today, Native Americans oversee the few remaining boarding schools, which offer an alternative education for young Indigenous students.

[41] *Yamástas* is Steptoe Butte in Eastern Washington near the Idaho border. It is a holy place to many Plateau people, including the Palouse. Tribal elders including Mary Jim, Andrew George, Emily Peone, and Gilbert Minthorn have shared accounts of the sacred mountain. In 2024 at the American Philosophical Society in Philadelphia, we found a copy of a translation given by a native elder in 1930 to a linguist about the sacred mountain. In 1982, Emily Peone, a Palouse elder living on the Colville Reservation, provided her version of the story. It is reprinted in Scheuerman and Trafzer, *River Song*, 137-138.

[42] The statement by Carrie Jim Schuster speaks of the independence and mobility of Palouse people. See Scheuerman and Trafzer, *River Song*, xi-xv.

Some of the movement of Palouse people from reservation to reservation and to places on the Columbia Plateau, see Trafzer and Scheuerman, *The Snake River-Palouse*, 175-191.

[43] Andrew, like other *twáti*, had the ability to use his spiritual power to heal and help others. However, he also had power to harm others if he chose to do so. During the past years of research among Plateau people, Trafzer and Scheuerman have never learned of Andrew George using his power to harm anyone. Quite the opposite. Accounts about Andrew suggest he used his power to heal others and contribute positively to their wellbeing.

[44] Oral Interview with Andrew George by Clifford E. Trafzer, Richard D. Scheuerman, and Lee Ann Smith, November 15, 1980, Yakama Reservation, Authors' Collections. Scheuerman and Trafzer, *River Song*, 74.

[45] Ibid.; Scheuerman and Trafzer, *River Song*, 74. For a discussion of learning through the oral tradition and repetitive stories as explained by Alex Saluskin, see Fisher, "This I Know from the Old People," 13.

[46] Oral Interview with Andrew George by Clifford E. Trafzer, Richard D. Scheuerman, and Lee Ann Smith, November 15, 1980, Yakama Reservation, Authors' Collections; Scheuerman and Trafzer, *River Song*, 74.

[47] Ibid., *River Song*, xii.

[48] Oral Interview with Andrew George by Clifford E. Trafzer, Richard D. Scheuerman, and Lee Ann Smith, November 15, 1980, Yakama Reservation, Authors' Collections.

[49] Oral Interview with Andrew George by Clifford E. Trafzer, Richard D. Scheuerman, and Lee Ann Smith, November 15, 1980, Yakama Reservation, Authors' Collections.

[50] Ibid., *River Song*, 74; Oral Interview with Andrew George by Clifford E. Trafzer, Richard D. Scheuerman, and Lee Ann Smith, November 15, 1980, Yakama Reservation, Authors' Collections.

[51] Larry Eddy was a leading Chemehuevi singer and elder on the Colorado River Indian Reservation. In March 2016, Trafzer had an informal conversation with him that lasted all day, which included a discussion of his grandfather, Dutch Eddy who was a prominent Nuwuvi healer. Both men have walked on, but Larry told Trafzer that he watched his grandfather perform a healing ceremony on the Colorado River Reservation near the banks of the Colorado River. Dutch Eddy sang and sang until Larry saw a bat, a spirit bat, fly into the camp but some distance from Dutch who continued to sing. According to Larry, the bat wanted to be noticed and was attracted to the singing, which was about the bat. The bat finally worked its way toward Dutch, and stopped when it reached his feet. Dutch, who was sitting on a log singing, quickly reached

down and grabbed the bat. With his familiar in hand, Dutch could do the healing. During his life, Dutch Eddy told a few people, primarily his family about his familiar, which lived in the mountains west of the reservation on the California side of the Colorado River. Another healer, Kenneth Coosewoon, was Comanche. He had no identifiable familiar. He believed that his healing power came directly from the Grandfather Creator. For more information about Kenneth and his healing experiences, see Clifford E. Trafzer, et. al., *Comanche Medicine Man* (Camano Island, Washington: Coyote Hill Press, 2015). Normally, Indigenous healers do not discuss their spirit helpers or familiars, but during a discussion with Cliff Trafzer, Chemehuevi elder Larry Eddy shared about his grandfather's spirit helper, namely a bat.

[52] Clifford E. Trafzer, ed., *Earth Song, Sky Spirit: Short Stories of the Contemporary Native American Experience* (New York: Doubleday, 1993), 1-4.

[53] Ibid; Oral interview with Josiah Pinkham by Clifford E. Trafzer, July 2008, Oklahoma City, Oklahoma, Authors' Collections.

[54] Oral interview with Josiah Pinkham by Clifford E. Trafzer, July 2008, Oklahoma City, Oklahoma, Authors' Collections.

[55] Ibid.

[56] Scheuerman and Trafzer, *River Song*, xiv.

[57] These words or similar words are found in treaties of the Northwest, including the Yakama, Umatilla, and Nez Perce Treaties of 1855.

[58] Oral Interview with Andrew George by Clifford E. Trafzer, Richard D. Scheuerman, and Lee Ann Smith, November 15, 1980, Yakama Reservation, Authors' Collections.

[59] According to the story, Salmon Chief beat Rattlesnake so hard on the head that his head became smashed, flattened by the beating the snake received.

[60] Oral Interview with Andrew George by Clifford E. Trafzer, Richard D. Scheuerman, and Lee Ann Smith, November 15, 1980, Yakama Reservation, Authors' Collections. While teaching the history of Northwestern Indians at Washington State University, Trafzer shared this account of salmon's poison with his class. One student, a Nez Perce fisher from the Colville Reservation, spoke up to tell the class that the story is true. He turned up one long sleeve of his shirt and showed everyone the injury he had received from the bite of a salmon.

[61] Trafzer, ed., *Grandmother, Grandfather, and Old World: Tamánwit Ku Súkat and Traditional Native American Narratives from the Columbia Plateau*, 107-109.

[62] Ibid.

[63] Ibid.

[64] Scheuerman and Trafzer, *River Song*, 74.

[65] Scheuerman and Trafzer, *River Song*, 45-58. Contemporary Palouse-Paiute elder Wilson Wewa of the Warm Springs Reservation of Oregon wrote, "Richard and Clifford sought through their work to visit descendants living in all these places and piece together a fuller understanding of their survival into our modern era. In this way, they also came to know some of the last people who had grown up in the old way there along the rivers—elders who were very mindful of our heritage, like Mary Jim and Andrew George."

[66] It is highly advised for researchers to make personal contact with tribal cultural and educational program directors as well as tribal elders. Some tribal websites direct researchers to cultural and educational committees or to elders' committees. Researchers may start there to reach out to tribes to begin relationships. Indigenous elders are amazing teachers. At times, researchers with little experience working with tribal people and authorities may be reluctant to reach out and engage the people. However, If tribal elders decide to share and teach with you, the researcher will be enriched with new and revealing knowledge. Researchers much check with tribes before their visits to see if the tribe has posted protocols. If so, they must follow them. It is prudent to inform the directors of tribal cultural and educational programs about the nature of research projects and how the research will benefit tribal people. After conducting oral histories, it is advised to send copies of the work to the tribal consultant. If that person agrees, the researcher might also provide copies of interviews and all work with programs and tribal archives.

[67] The book was published in January 1975 as part of the Consortium of Johnson O'Malley and Region IV of Washington state.

[68] Mary Jim, "Echo Mountains at Palouse," in Beavert, ed., *Anakú Iwachá: Yakama Legends and Stories*, 195-196.

[69] Ibid. Researchers may overlook a very limited-edition book edited by an Indigenous scholar and elder like Virginia Beavert. In the past, some tribes and tribal scholars wrote highly significant works that university scholars might overlook or consider insignificant. It is very important to search out past publications by tribes and tribal members as well as local historical societies as part of the research. Scholars must also investigate tribal archives if they exist and are open to non-tribal members.

[70] Historian Lee Ann Smith traveled to the Yakama Reservation with us during our research trips. Today, she is an Instructor of European, American, and World history at California State University, San Bernardino, Chaffee College, and San Bernardino Valley College.

[71] Clifford E. Trafzer and Richard D. Scheuerman, *Renegade Tribe: The Palouse Indians and the Invasion of the Inland Pacific Northwest* (Pullman, WSU

Press 1986), a title approved by Palouse elders who characterized themselves and their ancestors as renegades against the United States. The second edition (2016) bears a new title, *The Snake River-Palouse and the Invasion of the Inland Pacific Northwest*.

[72] Oral Interview with Mary Jim by Clifford E. Trafzer and Richard D. Scheuerman, November 10-17, 1979, Yakama Reservation, Authors' Collections.

[73] Ibid., 81-85, 91, 134; Scheuerman and Trafzer, *River Song*, 48-49, 52-53, 57. Estamlóot was born about 1845 along Snake River, and his name was a long-used Jim family name. After peacefully meeting with soldiers, Colonel Cornelius and the Oregon Volunteers murdered Walla Walla Chief Peo Peo Mox Mox (Yellow Bird) and desecrated his body.

[74] White soldiers and settlers believed the colonel had rescued the boy so he could become "civilized" and a Christian.

[75] Scheuerman and Trafzer, *River Song*, 3, 52-53.

[76] Ibid.,3, 49-50, 52-53, 107-108, 132; Trafzer and Scheuerman, *The Snake River-Palouse*, 4-7, 104-105, 154, 161-162, 166; Karson, ed., Wiyáxayxt Wiyáakaa'awn, 30-32, 43, 46, 62, 85, 8. The horses bred on the Columbia Plateau were known to be strong, smart, and durable with tough hooves. People often referred to these horses as Cayuses. The Palouse were fond of breeding horses with spotted rumps or spots about their bodies. They were called "a Palouse horse," origin of the name Appaloosa. In 2024, Roberta (Bobbie) Conner provided an oral interview about the significance of horses and buffalo to Plateau people, including her tribes, Cayuse and Nez Perce. The oral history is on file at Tamástslikt Institute, Umatilla Indian Reservation, Pendleton, Oregon. Hereafter cited as Conner, "Horses and Buffalo." Conner is the long-time director of the Institute.

[77] Ibid., Conner, "Horses and Buffalo."

[78] Oral interviews with Mary Jim by Clifford E. Trafzer and Richard Scheuerman, April 2, 1977, May 1, 1977, November 10, 1979, November 17, 1979, April 25, 1980, Yakama Reservation, Authors' Collections.

[79] Oral Interview with Mary Jim by Clifford E. Trafzer and Richard D. Scheuerman, November 10-17, 1979, Yakama Reservation, Authors' Collections.

[80] Ibid.

[81] Scheuerman and Trafzer, *River Song*, 48-49.

[82] Ibid.

[83] Ibid., 49-50.

[84] Oral Interview with Mary Jim by Clifford E. Trafzer and Richard D. Scheuerman, November 10-17, 1979, Yakama Reservation, Authors' Collections.

⁸⁵ Ibid.; Karson, ed., Wiyáxayxt Wiyáakaa'awn,15, 23, 79, 124, 128, 224, 145, 251.

⁸⁶ Oral interviews with Mary Jim by Clifford E. Trafzer and Richard Scheuerman, April 2, 1977, May 1, 1977, November 10, 1979, November 17, 1979, April 25, 1980, Yakama Reservation, Authors' Collections. For more information on the *Washani* Faith and *tamánwit*, see Karson, Wiyáxayxt Wiyáakaa'awn, 3, 15, 17, 23, 73, 77-79, 88, 124, 128, 224, 245, 248-249, 251; Beavert, *The Way It Was*, iii, x-xii; Trafzer, *The Nez Perce*, 18-21.

⁸⁷ Scheuerman and Trafzer, *River Song*, 76.

⁸⁸ Ibid., 50.

⁸⁹ Karson, Wiyáxayxt Wiyáakaa'awn, 3, 15, 17, 23, 73, 77-79, 88, 124, 128, 224, 245, 248-249, 251.

⁹⁰ Scheuerman and Trafzer, *River Song*, xi.

⁹¹ Gerald McMaster and Clifford E. Trafzer, *Native Universe: Voices of Indian America* (Washington, D.C.: National Museum of the American Indian and National Geographic Society, 2004), 16, 66, 70, 239, 264, 266-272, 275. This volume contains many references to specific foods found in the native universe.

⁹² Ibid.

⁹³ Oral interviews with Mary Jim by Clifford E. Trafzer and Richard Scheuerman, April 2, 1977, May 1, 1977, November 10, 1979, November 17, 1979, April 25, 1980, Yakama Reservation, Authors' Collections.

⁹⁴ Schuster, "*Kukyáma Tamánwit*," unpublished manuscript (2024). For information on music at Chemawa Indian School in Salem, Oregon, see Melissa D. Parkhurst, *To Win the Indian's Heart: Music at Chemawa Indian School* (Corvallis: Oregon State University Press, 2014).

⁹⁵ A rare photograph of Mary Jim's home on Snake River appears in Scheuerman and Trafzer, *River Song*, p. 48.

⁹⁶ Scheuerman and Trafzer, *River Song*, 49.

⁹⁷ Ibid., 54, 55, 57.

⁹⁸ After the passage of the Native American Graves Protection and Repatriation Act (1990) the Palouse and other tribes of the Columbia Plateau negotiated with Washington State University to rebury the ancestors whom archaeologists had removed from graves along Snake River. In 2006 the university returned 150 Ancestors to the earth along the banks of Snake River at Lyons Ferry State Park. Many tribal representatives participated in the reburial, which concluded a horrific Indigenous chapter, especially for Mary Jim, Andrew George, and their families.

⁹⁹ To make a canoe burial, the people cut the canoe halfway from stem to

stern, laid the body inside half of the canoe, then inverted the other half of the canoe over the first, thereby covering the body.

[100] Scheuerman and Trafzer, *River Song*, 54-54.

[101] Oral interviews with Mary Jim by Clifford E. Trafzer and Richard Scheuerman, April 2, 1977, May 1, 1977, November 10, 1979, Authors' Collections; Scheuerman and Trafzer, *River Song*, 57.

[102] Oral interviews with Mary Jim by Clifford E. Trafzer and Richard Scheuerman, April 2, 1977, May 1, 1977, November 10, 1979, Authors' Collections.

[103] Scheuerman and Trafzer, *River Song*, 55.

[104] In 1978, Trafzer consulted about excavations on Snake River with archaelogists who stated that all the items taken from Snake River were in bags and boxes but did not reveal where the items were stored or how to access them; they made no reference to the exhumed human remains. When Trafzer investigated further about their storage, a senior professor in anthropology told him to stop investigating or he would endeavor to prevent Trafzer from advancing to associate professor and tenure. Trafzer continued his inquiry but to no avail. Ultimately, tribal people brought about the return of remains and patrimony for their reburial in 2006 after the passage of NAGPRA.

[105] Scheuerman and Trafzer, *River Song*, 55.

[106] Ibid., 54.

[107] Mary Jim often explained her responsibility, Harry Jim's, and past elders to protect the graves of their people. We visited with Mary after Mount St. Helens exploded. She said that the mountain had erupted as a message from Mother Earth that Native Americans were not acting correctly in accordance with *tamánwit*. The earth, she said, was conveying a message to regional Indigenous people to follow the old rules, including those relating to the care of the dead and their resting places. Oral interviews with Mary Jim by Clifford E. Trafzer and Richard Scheuerman, April 2, 1977, May 1, 1977, November 10 and 17, 1979, April 25, 1980, Yakama Reservation, Authors' Collections.

[108] Some archaeologists who excavated the graves on Big Island became ill. After consulting medical doctors, one of the archaeologists visited with the Jim family and Indigenous healers to ask for help, to undo the negative power caused by his excavation of graves. The healer explained that it was too late. The Native Americans and archaeologist attributed the illness to his actions in removing burials. The medicine person told the archaeologist that he could do nothing to cure his illness. Shortly afterwards, he walked on.

[109] Trafzer and Scheuerman, *Snake River-Palouse*, xii.

[110] Scheuerman and Trafzer, *River Song*, xi.

[111] Schuster, "Kukyáma Tamánwit."

APPENDIX

COLUMBIA PLATEAU
TRIBAL SUSTAINABILITY PRINCIPLES

The National Council of Teachers of English invited a presentation on Indigenous Columbia Plateau values at the organization's national conference in Washington, D.C. in November 2014. This event provided an opportunity to share with educators from across the country core principles of sustainability relevant to teachers and others. For the First Peoples of the Columbia Plateau, these beliefs have long guided a way of life. Respected nineteenth-century Plateau spiritual leaders like the Snake River-Palouse Washani *headmen Thomash and Wolf, Walla Walla Chief Homly, Kotaiaqan among the Yakama, and the Wanapum prophet Smohalla expressed these beliefs through traditional* Wáshat *ceremonies and in meetings with government officials. Consideration of these ideas through teachings of the elders about traditions, oral literature, and environmental understandings offers a legacy of wellbeing for future generations.*

PERVASIVE SPIRITUALITY

Human experience is linked to sacred obligations within nature. Reliance upon Mother Earth for sustenance does not assume we exist apart from our "place" within the environmental system. For example, our Indian names for family and band clusters are derived from the suffix –pam, or "people of" with Indigenous reference to a place. Human beings are to be stewards or proprietors (vs. owners) of creation. Humanity exists in a covenant relationship, or sacred trust (*ahtow'*), with the Creator through which sustenance is provided to people, animals, and plants. This is what the Plateau chiefs of the nineteenth century meant when they spoke to government officials about the "law" (*tamánwit*).

ENVIRONMENTAL KNOWLEDGE

Natural resources are respectfully used and managed through intimate understandings of environmental systems, native species, and agricultural practices. The desire to get more than one needs leads individuals, groups, and even nations to harm land and life. The health of individuals and culture is related to the health of the environment—plains and forests, streams and rivers, beaches and oceans. Experiential knowledge further involves detailed cosmological lore related to hunting and fishing, gathering and cultivation, and realms of meteorological and astronomical understanding. Elders refer to geographic features as relational subjects (e.g., "We lived on Snake River"), rather than impersonal objects.

White Bluffs at Hanford Reach
John Clement Photograph

LANGUAGE AND MORAL LITERATURE

Words contain special force implicit in sounds associated with natural forces, life forms, and landscapes (e.g., fire, wind, animals, personal names) and storytelling fosters understanding of experience. Cultural knowledge and wisdom transmitted through myth (ancient), tale (experiential), lore (anecdotal), and oral history provides practical and symbolic means to meaningfully relate to place and culture. These experiences develop moral sensibilities for respect, stewardship, reciprocity (sharing), cooperation, hospitality, and cleanliness. The stories are meant for all time and for all generations, and each time they are told, they offer a creative force that links today with yesterday. Songs express appreciation for the "law" that descended to Earth and put all things in existence commemorating the sacrifice of creation for humanity. Elders teach and maintain cultural memory to guide youth and sustain natural resources for future well-being. Lessons and experiences for personal identity and affiliation develop through the stages of life (e.g., fire-keeper [child] > hunter [adolescent] > trader [adult] > etc.), and impart responsibilities to family, clan, and community.

CEREMONY AND CELEBRATION

Songs, dances, feasts, rites and other ceremonies recognize and commemorate relationships with one another, within families, among generations, and between peoples and creation. As Mary Jim observed, "The First Foods Feast shows the Creator's sacred way. Start with water (*kúš*), then the chiefs of the creatures: salmon (*núsux*) for fish and venison or deer (*yáamaš*) for animals, then the plants (bitterroot/*piyáxi*) and fruits (currants/*khánən*)." Ceremonies offer thanksgiving and teach obligations to animals and plants, landscapes and waters, and the Creator to reveal our place and responsibilities in the web of life.

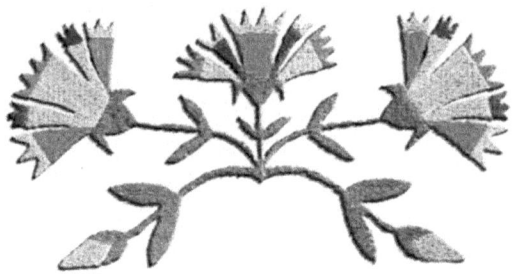

ARTISTIC EXPRESSION

Baskets, bags, clothing, gear, and other material goods are made from natural materials. They are generally decorated with motifs associated with their particular use, place of origin, or individual or family identity that impart a sacred influence beyond symbolic value. For example, Kotaiaqan's sacred colors were white, symbolizing earthly light and unseen spirit; blue (placed in the center) for water and sky; and yellow for the heavenly light of the spirit world. Specific practices are taught for the gathering and processing of plant materials and are often accompanied by songs and ceremonies. Through these preparations and in the actual weaving, sewing, and beading, individuals learn about tribal culture, family ancestors, and individual spirituality.

CYCLICAL TIME

Aspects of physical and spiritual experience reoccur in life cycles that transcend time and circumstance not bound by linear progression. Time exists in a dimension beyond the course of chronological events. Happenings from the age of myth and personal qualities of persons from former generations are sometimes revealed in dreams or in the sounds of nature for those who listen, and lived out in contemporary experience. The hemp string "time ball" (*ititamat*), literally a "day counter," or calendar, was tied with tiny markers of colored stones, bones, beads, and cloth to record significant events throughout one's lifetime, and ultimately would be buried with the owner. Just as events from an individual's "season" might touch upon another from a different time and place, so humanity's wisdom and experience may intersect through power of a sacred word, story, creature, or event.

RESPONSIBLE INNOVATION

Change can be beneficial when promoting the well-being of humans within the natural world system and among other peoples. Conflicts with the dominant culture have often arisen when such constraints are ignored in the name of short-term gain or perceived higher needs. Plateau political leaders ("chiefs," or *miyúux*) like Kamiakin welcomed missionaries and adopted such agricultural and pastoral innovations as the raising of grains, crop irrigation, and selective breeding of livestock. Spiritual leaders ("shamans," "medicine men," or *twáti*) like Thomash or teachers (*iyánča*) like Smohalla spoke of the family of all mankind, and accepted technological progress within the limits of moral obligations to *Náami Pyap's* creation. The discipline of restraint has both physical and spiritual dimensions. It is the cultural means to prevent insatiable consumption that can wreak long-lasting destruction. Government engineers sought to impound the region's entire Columbia-Snake River system for hydroelectricity threatening the Fish Nations, and some scientists sought to keep ancient human remains indefinitely in spite of federal legislation and moral imperatives for repatriation and burial.

BIBLIOGRAPHY

Oral Histories

Gordon Fisher. June 19, 2000; July 24, 2008; December 28, 2009 (Lapwai, Idaho), June 16, 2006 (Lyons Ferry, Washington).

Andrew George. November 15, 1980 (Toppenish, Washington); November 11, 1981 (Wapato, Washington).

Mary Jim. May 1, 1977; April 1-2, 1979; November 17, 1979; August 12, 1980; February 21, 1985 (Parker, Washington).

Antoine Minthorn. January 6-7, 2024 (Pendleton, Oregon).

Thomas Morning Owl. September 24, 2024 (Pendleton, Oregon).

Sam Pambrun. June 13, 2019; January 6, 2024 (Pendleton, Oregon).

Ike Patrick. May 8, 1981 (Mission, Oregon).

Emily Peone. April 4, 1981; November 5, 1981; April 30, 1982 (Nespelem, Washington).

Carrie Jim Schuster. September 21-22, 2017; September 1, 2018 (Parker, Washington).

Joe Thompson. May 9, 1981 (Mission, Oregon).

Marjorie Waheneka. November 19, 2024 (Pendleton, Oregon).

Wilson Wewah. November 27, 2023 (Pendleton, Oregon).

David Wolf. November 25, 2023; September 24, 2025 (Mission, Oregon).

Manuscript Collections

Eastern Washington University, Archives and Special Collections, Cheney: Winans and Kingston Collections.

Federal Records Center, Seattle, Washington: Colville Agency Records, Simms Letters, Yakima Agency Records.

Gonzaga University, Foley Library, Spokane, Washington: Ray Collection.

National Archives, Washington, D.C.: Indian Claims Commission Dockets 161, 222, 224; Records of the Bureau of Indian Affairs; Records Related to Negotiations of Ratified Treaties.

National Anthropological Museum, Washington, D.C.: Sohon and National Congress of American Indian Collections.

Spalding Center Museum, Spalding, Idaho: Spalding-Allen Collection.

Northwest Museum of Arts & Culture, Spokane, Washington: Davis, Doty, Ruby, and Harder Collections.

Oregon Province Archives of the Society of Jesus, Crosby Library, Gonzaga University, Spokane, Washington: Cataldo, DeSmet, Joset, and Kowrach Collections

Tamástslikt Cultural Institute, Umatilla Indian Reservation, Pendleton, Oregon: Treaty of 1855 Exhibit.

University of Oregon, Special Collections, Eugene: Palmer Collection, Nez Perce Agency Letterbook.

University of Queensland, Department of Anthropology, Graceville: Rigsby Papers.

University of Washington Suzzallo Library, Special Collections, Seattle: Haller, Jacobs, Stevens, and Swan Collections.

Washington State Historical Society Research Center, Tacoma, Washington: Ankeny and Milroy Collections.

Washington State University Holland and Terrell Library, Manuscripts, Archives and Special Collections, Pullman: Brown, DeSmet, Deutsch, Horan, Kuykendal, McGregor, McWhorter, Oliphant, Simms, Sutherland, White, and Winans Collections.

Yakama Nation Heritage Cultural Center, Yakama Indian Reservation, Toppenish, Washington: Oral History Collection.

Yakima Valley Regional Library, Yakima, Washington: Relander Collection.

Books and Manuscripts

Bancroft, H. H. *History of Washington, Idaho, and Montana, 1845-1889*, in Works, Vol. 31. San Francisco, 1890.

Brown, Roberta Stringham and Killen, Patricia O'Connell. *Selected Letters of A. M. A. Blanchet, Bishop of Walla Walla & Nesqualy*. Seattle: University of Washington Press, 2013.

Brown, William C. *The Indian Side of the Story*. Spokane: C. W. Hill Printing Company, 1961.

Burns, Robert Ignatius. *The Jesuits and the Indian Wars of the Northwest*. New Haven: Yale University Press, 1966.

Chalfant, Stuart A. *Interior Salish and Eastern Washington Indians*. 4 vols. New York: Garland Publishing, 1974.

Clark, Ella. *Indian Legends of the Pacific Northwest*. Berkeley: University of California Press, 1960.

Clark, Frank B. *History of the Farm near Umapine, Oregon which was operated by the Hudson's Bay Company.* Unpublished manuscript, Penrose Library Archives, Whitman College, 1938.

Colville Confederated Tribes. *The Year of the Coyote: Centennial Celebration, July 2, 1872.* Nespelem, 1972.

Curtis, Edward S. *The North American Indian.* Cambridge, Massachusetts: The University Press, 1911.

Creighton, J. J. *Indian Summers: Washington State College and the Nespelem Art Colony, 1937-1941.* Pullman: Washington State University, 2000.

Deloria, Jr., Vine, ed. *American Indian Policy in the Twentieth Century.* Norman: University of Oklahoma Press, 1985.

Drury, Clifford M. *Marcus and Narcissa Whitman and the Opening of Old Oregon.* Vols. I & II. Glendale, California: The Arthur H. Clark Company, 1973.

Frey, Rodney. *Landscape Traveled by Coyote and Crane: The World of the Schitsu/umsh (Coeur d'Alene Indians).* Seattle: University of Washington Press, 2005.

Frey, Rodney, ed. *Stories that Make the World: Oral Literature of the Indian Peoples of the Inland Northwest.* Norman: University of Oklahoma Press, 1995.

Gibson, James R.; *Farming the Frontier, the Agriculture Opening of the Oregon Country 1786-1846,* Seattle: University of Washington Press, 1986.

Gibson, James R. *Lifeline of the Oregon Country, The Fraser-Columbia Brigade System, 1811-1847.* Vancouver: University of British Columbia Press, 1997.

Haines, Francis. *Appaloosa, The Spotted Horse in Art and History.* Austin: University of Texas Press, 1963.

Harmon, Alexandra, ed. *The Power of Promises: Rethinking Indian Treaties in the Pacific Northwest.* Seattle, University of Washington Press, 2008.

Hunn, Eugene, with James Selam. *Nch'i-Wana: The Big River, Mid-Columbia Indians and Their Land.* Seattle: University of Washington Press, 1990.

Kamiakin, Tomio. "Chief Kamiakin." L. V. McWhorter Collection, MASC, Washington State University, Pullman.

Manring, B. F. *Conquest of the Coeur d'Alenes, Spokanes, and Palouses.* Spokane, Washington: Inland Printing Company, 1912.

Miller, Christopher L. *Prophetic Worlds: Indians and Whites on the Columbia Plateau.* New Brunswick, New Jersey: Rutgers University Press, 1985.

Mullan, John. *Report on the Construction of a Military Road from Fort Walla Walla to Fort Benton.* Washington, D.C.: Government Printing Office, 1863.

Nichols, M. Leona. *The Mantle of Elias: The Story of Fathers Blanchet and Demers in Early Oregon.* Portland: Binfords & Mort, 1941.

Pambrun, Andrew D. *Sixty Years on the Frontier in the Pacific Northwest.* Fairfield, Washington: Ye Galleon Press, [c. 1893] 1978.

Raffan, James; *Emperor of the North; Sir George Simpson and the Remarkable Story of the Hudson's Bay Company.* New York: Harper-Collins Publishers, 2007.

Reimers, Henry [with Wes Lloyd]. *The Secret Saga of Five Sack* [George Lucas]. Ye Galleon Press, 1975.

Relander, Click. *Drummers and Dreamers.* Caldwell, Idaho: The Caxton Printers, Ltd., 1956.

Rigsby, Bruce. "Changing Property Relations in land and Resources in the Southern Plateau." Unpublished typescript, BRC, UQ, 2006.

Roe, Frank. *The Indian and the Horse.* Norman: University of Oklahoma Press, 1968.

Scheuerman, Richard D., and Michael O. Finley. *Finding Chief Kamiakin: The Life and Legacy of a Northwest Patriot.* Pullman: Washington State University Press (2008).

Scheuerman, Richard D. *Palouse Country: A Land and Its People.* Walla Walla, Washington: Color Press, 1994.

Seaburg, William R. and Laurel Sercomb, eds. *Folk-Tales of the Coast Salish.* Collected and Edited by Thelma Adamson. Lincoln: University of Nebraska Press, 2009.

Sohon, Gustavus. "Records of the Walla Walla Council, 30th May 1855, Translated in the Language of the Spokan Indians," n.d., Manuscript 4306-c, National Anthropological Archives, Washington, D.C.

Splawn, A. J. *Ka-Mi-Akin, Last Hero of the Yakimas.* Portland, Oregon: Stationary and Printing Company, 1917.

Stern, Theodore. *Chiefs & Change in the Oregon Country: Indian Relations at Fort Nez Percés,1818 1855.* Corvallis: Oregon State University Press, 1996.

———. *Chiefs & Traders: Indian Relations at Fort Nez Percés, 1818-1855.* Corvallis: Oregon State University Press, 1993.

Stevens, Hazard. *The Life of Isaac Ingalls Stevens.* 2 vols. Boston: Houghton, Mifflin and Company, 1901.

Stevens, Isaac I. *Narrative and Final Report of Explorations for a Route for a Pacific Railroad, Near the Forty-Seventh and Forty-Ninth Parallels of North Latitude from St. Paul to Puget Sound.* Washington, D.C.: Government Printing Office, 1855, 1860.

———. *Washington and Oregon War Claims.* Washington, D.C., 1858.

Trafzer, Clifford E. *Earth Song, Sky Spirit: Short Stories of the Contemporary Native American Experience.* New York: Doubleday, 1992.

Trafzer, Clifford E., and Richard D. Scheuerman. *Renegade Tribe: The Palouse Indians and the Invasion of the Inland Pacific Northwest.* Pullman: Washington State University Press, 1986.

Trafzer, Clifford E., ed. *Indians, Superintendents, and Councils: Northwestern Indian Policy, 1850 1855.* Lanham, Maryland: University Press of America, 1986.

Walker, Deward E., Jr., ed. *Handbook of North American Indians.* Vol. 12 (Plateau). Washington, D.C.: Smithsonian Institution, 1998.

Wilkes, Charles. *Narrative of the United States Exploring Expedition During the Years 1838, 1839, 1840, 1841, and 1842.* Philadelphia: Lea and Blanchard, 1845.

Winthrop, Theodore. *The Canoe and the Saddle, or Klalam and Klickitat.* Tacoma, Washington: John H. Williams, 1913.

Yanan, Eileen, ed., *Coyote and the Colville.* Omak, Washington: St. Mary's Mission, 1971.

Articles and Reports

Ballard, Arthur C. "Mythology of Southern Puget Sound," *University of Washington Publications in Anthropology* 3:2 (December 1929): 31-150.

Beall, Thomas B. "Pioneer Reminiscences." *Washington Historical Quarterly* 8 (1917): 83-90.

Bischoff, William N. "The Yakima Campaign of 1856." *Mid-America* 31 (1949):163-208

_____. "The Yakima Indian War, 1855-56, a Problem in Research," *Pacific Northwest Quarterly* 41 (1950):162-169.

Brown, W. C. "Life of Owhi is Epic," *Wenatchee Daily World*, February 21, 1928.

Burns, Robert Ignatius. "Pere Joset's Account of the Indian War of 1858." *Pacific Northwest Quarterly* 38 (1947):285-314.

Chadwick, S. J. "Colonel Steptoe's Battle." *Washington Historical Quarterly* 2 (1907-08):333-43.

Clark, Stanley J. "The Nez Perces in Exile." *Oregon Historical Quarterly* 36 (1935):14-59.

Coonc, Elizabeth Ann. "Reminiscences of a Pioneer Woman." *Washington Historical Quarterly* 8 (1917):14-21.

Deutsch, Herman J. "Indian and White in the Inland Empire: The Contest for the Land, 1880-1912." *Pacific Northwest Quarterly* 47 (1956):44-51.

Elliot, T. C. "Steptoe Butte and Steptoe Battle-field." *Washington Historical Quarterly* 18 (1927): 243-253.

Fisher, Andrew. H. "'This I Know from the Old People:' Yakama Indian Treaty Rights as Oral Tradition." *Montana. The Magazine of Western History* 49, No. 1 (1999):468-492.

Frush, Charles W. "A Trip from the Dalles of the Columbia, Oregon, to Fort Owen, Bitter Root Valley, Montana, in the Spring of 1858." *Contributions to the Historical Society of Montana* 2 (1896):337-42.

Garrecht, Francis A. "An Indian Chief." *Washington Historical Quarterly* 19 (1928):167-78.

Gibbs, George, et. al. "Reports on the Indian Tribes of the Territory of Washington." *Secretary of War Reports of Explorations* 1 (1854):400-49.

Jacobs, Melville. "A Sketch of Northern Sahaptin Grammar." *University of Washington Publications in Anthropology* 4 (1931):83-292.

Kamiakin, Cleveland. "The Vision Quest." *Tác Titóoquan News* (March 2003), 5.

Lewis, William S., ed., "The Daughter of Angus MacDonald [Christina McDonald McKenzie Williams]," *Washington Historical Quarterly* 13 (1922):107-117.

MacMurray, J. W. "The Dreamers of the Columbia River Valley in Washington Territory." *Transactions of the Albany Institute* 11 (1887): 241-48.

McDermott, Paul D. and Ronald E. Grim. "The Artistic Views of Gustavus Sohon." *Columbia* (Summer 2002): 16-22.

McDonald, Angus. "A Few Items of the West." *Washington Historical Quarterly* 8 (1917):188-229.

Meany, Edmond S. ed. "Historic Gardens of Chief Kamiakin." *Washington Historical Quarterly* 9 (1918): 240.

Painter, Harry. "New Light on Chief Kamiakin." *Walla Walla Union Bulletin.* March 18, 1945.

Painter, Robert M., and William C. Painter. "Journals of the Indian War of 1855-1856." *Washington Historical Quarterly* 15 (1924):11-31.

_____. "The Indian War of 1858." *Washington Historical Quarterly* 2 (1908):237-40.

Ray, Verne. "Native Villages and Groupings of the Columbia Basin." *Pacific Northwest Quarterly* 27 (1936):99-152.

_____. "Tribes of the Columbia Confederacy, and the Palus." Plantiff's Exhibit No. 112, U. S. Court of Claims, Docket 261-70 (1973).

Richards, Kent. "Issac Stevens and Federal Military Power in Washington Territory." *Pacific Northwest Quarterly* 63 (1972):81-86.

Rigsby, Bruce, and Noel Rude. "Sketch of Sahaptin, a Sahaptian Language." *Handbook of North American Indians*. Vol. 17. Washington, D.C.: Smithsonian Institution, 1996.

Schuster, Helen H. "Yakima and Neighboring Groups." *Handbook of North American Indians*. Vol. 12. Washington, D.C.: Smithsonian Institution, 1998.

Sprague, Roderick. "The Meaning of 'Palouse.'" *Idaho Yesterdays* 12 (1968):22-27.

_____. "Palouse," *Handbook of North American Indians*. Edited by Deward Walker. Washington, D.C.: Smithsonian Institution, 1998.

Thompson, Albert. "The Early History of the Palouse River and Its Names." *Pacific Northwest Quarterly* 62 (1971):69-71.

Thompson, Erwin N. "Men and Events on the Lower Snake River." *Idaho Yesterdays* 5 (1961): 10-15.

Trafzer, Clifford E., and Richard D. Scheuerman, "The First Peoples of the Palouse Country." *Bunchgrass Historian* 8 (1890):3-18.

Wakeneka, Marjorie, "Indian Perspectives on Food and Culture." *Oregon Historical Quarterly* Vol 106, No. 3 (2015) 468-474.

INDEX

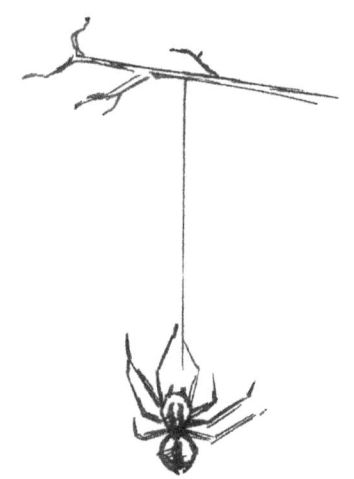